NO GOOD DEED GOES

UNPUNISHED

Or How to Lose Millions of Dollars in Future Oil Income because of Spineless Thieves

PATRICK BEASON

PAGE PUBLISHING
Conneaut Lake, PA

First originally published by Page Publishing 2024

ISBN 979-8-89157-166-2 (pbk)
ISBN 979-8-89157-178-5 (digital)

Printed in the United States of America

CONTENTS

The following elaborates on the reason behind writing this book.

First and maybe last, this book wouldn't have been possible if it was not for the theft of all those whom I had so richly rewarded with hundreds of thousands of dollars in income and several million dollars to the contract vendor. Writing this helps with a little release of pent-up anger but at the same time reminds me of all the treacherous and deceptive behaviors of my previous staff as well as the associates and contract vendors. In this book, I have discussed how these people took advantage of my generosity and made me lose several million dollars in future income. I will, no doubt, change my practices on hiring individuals and use data available on the web to ensure I don't end up with drug-addled people with criminal backgrounds anymore.

I have changed the names of the participants and projects in this book only to guard against litigation and protect the reprehensible guilty. Some people are deceased; any similarity to anyone or company is purely coincidental. I have always told people that if they want to start their own oil company, they don't have to steal my clients and projects. Typically, those who do things of that nature may end up facing prison or pushing dirt from the bottom up.

I want to express my gratitude to a few who helped me put all this together. First, I would like to mention Ronnie from Midland. We have developed a friendship over the years that I will always treasure.

Ronnie fielded many calls from my clients and proved to them that Gil was the one at fault. Ronnie had previously worked with Gil and discovered that he was a habitual liar with many federal convictions and did not feel bad about stealing from me and slandering me.

Lastly and most importantly, my bride, who for the last thirty-two years, has been reading my drafts of this book repeatedly. She helped me to keep this mostly "G-rated" while still allowing me to keep some Texas vernacular. So I would like to thank her for her contributions.

Here We Go

The story begins when I met with one of the most convincing con artists I ever met in the oil and gas sales industry. I guess the word *convincing* is the reason they are called con men. Charlie, a fellow I was working with at another sales shop, read an ad in the newspaper that a guy, "Jack," was looking for business partners.

We agreed to meet with this fellow at a local restaurant to discuss a deal. A few weeks later, we all agreed to start up our business with this guy; after all, he had a cool company name, and it was registered with the state. He was not a licensed Texas oil and gas operator, but we thought that was too soon to sign up for. After all, the future projects we intended to expand the company with were not in Texas. However, we did have a small Jacksboro, Texas, location to start the company with.

The presentation data was a joke as it was not at all professional, and it would be a lost cause to raise sufficient funds with this presentation. After all, the competition had professional graphic artists who had prepared their maps professionally. The geological data on the competitors' books kicked our butt with log cross sections proving various producing horizons and the thickness of each zone and 3D mapping.

To say the guy was cheap and greedy would be an absolute understatement. Jack's office was one of the apartments he had just moved out of in North Dallas with subpar office equipment and a postal mail center for the official office address. He proved to be of no help in the sales part of the company, and once again, all sales were solely my responsibility. There was no reason to attempt to sell the project because it was so weak. We had cheesy black-and-white maps that we colored in with graphic pencils to show the contrast between oil formations and gas zones. The geological write-up was weak, and we put all of it together in a cheesy cardboard three-hole punch binder.

Charlie was a very weak salesperson; and although he had made only some sales at our previous place, he did not do much here either, so his contribution was insignificant. As a matter of fact, I sold about 90 percent of the projects while the owner of the previous company sold probably 5 percent or maybe more that I didn't know about. Charlie did nothing as he was usually never at the office, and whenever he was in the office, he kept his bottle of bourbon company with him most of the time.

Charlie stayed with one of our previous sales shops until Jack had the geological write-up more complete on our new deal. I had sold most of the projects out from the other company and was waiting for this guy to complete the last of the wells we had just drilled. While waiting for the rest of the completion money to come in, we started our new deal. So I left to go to the new office. It was a big mistake as the guy stole $27,800 from me in commissions.

Jack doing a rewrite on the geological data was not helpful either because the presentation book was too weak; we scraped this for another prospect. We selected a lease in Iowa Park, Texas, which was very shallow; but I told Jack we needed more data to put in our book and that the presentation book had to be more on the professional side. This site had a bit more sizzle; it actually had some very famous oil and gas men that had drilled on the lease in the very distant past. That data is what I used to offset some of the wells. The production wasn't very impressive, but it did have daily oil production. We started looking for another site to drill and found some areas in Illinois. We started the new project with a fair start. Russ's crew wasn't very strong in raising money. I guess they followed their leader's sales ability but not much talent either.

I later learned that the owner of the previous company wasn't paying attention to the drill bit going down the wellbore, and the drill rig caused him to have a severely deviated hole. As a matter of fact, one of the logging crew members told me the borehole looked like it had a horseshoe in the middle. So when they were running the open hole logs on the well, the gamma tool got stuck in the hole. As it was a radioactive device, they had to cut the wireline off and close the well in. They left it cemented in about a one-hundred-foot radius ten feet deep area around the wellbore so the gamma tool wouldn't contaminate the area. I understood it was going to be a damn good well. It served him right for being an insolent cheat. Much money was wasted on this well. I don't know whether it was because he didn't care or possibly before I got there to help him close business, he had sold some of the well maybe more than he should have. So when I started getting some of my people into the project, the entire program may have been oversold. The best way to cure that problem was to declare a dry hole having problems during completion.

This jackass called the IRS and reported to them that I wasn't paying my taxes because he reported that I had received more income than I actually did as I challenged him on the $27,800 that I never received. I did get a phone call from a guy claiming to be with the IRS, and about four weeks later, I got a letter to bring my files to their Dallas office. It turned out to be their show as they claimed the write-off I was claiming for sales lead expenses and travel to the field wasn't allowed since I didn't own the company paying for the drilling. He even tried to report more income on IRS tax forms than he actually paid me. Of course, that was simple to dispute. However, his lying about his company actually being the responsible party purchasing sales leads did end up costing me a disallowance on my write-off on taxes of about $10,000, and I ended up paying the IRS $10,000 plus penalties.

Jack continued with advertising for business partners and even brought a few guys in, none of whom could close a door with the instructions on the other side. So my best recommendation to Jack was to put these two guys in charge, and I would go my own way, or he could dump these two guys and put some money in an office and focus on our company so we could start up a real sales crew and train everyone how to close.

To my surprise, we did start a crew and went on to raise minor amounts of money and drill a few projects, none of which had very much success. However, we did drill and complete wells; we started drilling in Pike County, Illinois. The landowner was absolutely a wise guy, trying to tell us how to bring the wells in. We let him think he was directing us when in reality, his suggestions were absolutely asinine. We completed the well according to generally accepted field standards that I knew would be productive. I knew the well would be one of the most successful gas wells in the immediate area.

We sent one of Jack's new business partners, Russ, whom he hired to start another money-raising crew to Illinois to oversee the drilling of the wells. Even though this guy had some investors in the project, only five out of thirty-two people, Russ needed money to go to the site. Russ, however, stole the Illinois leases from me with Jack's help. Jack signed over the leases to Russ's company without my permission, signature, or knowledge. I didn't learn of this betrayal until I attempted to make assignments for my clients.

I could not convince Jack and Russ that the proper thing to do was to reassign the leases back to the company that Jack and I were partners in. I told Jack to be ready to get a suit filed against Russ and his company, but Jack assured me he would take care of the issues with Russ. However, that never transpired. If I filed suit against Russ and his company, Jack would be included since he owned a majority interest in Russ's company. To add insult to injury, I had been financing Russ's and Jack's business unbeknownst to me. They also had the audacity to expect me to continue paying their expenses. I gave Jack chance after chance to quit doing business in his usual and typical unethical way, but he squandered every chance I gave him as he was an excellent con man.

After we finished drilling, the landowner wanted to burn the brush pile we created by clearing the drill site. We wanted to push the pile into the reserve pit and cover it with dirt. My way was the traditional and safest, but his plan was a bit different, and he felt it was better. He drenched the brush pile with gasoline but still had the gas can in his hand when he threw the lighter into the pile. We had cautioned him to stand farther back, but he considered himself a pro who had done this several times before.

Guess what happened next? He stood too close to the fire, still holding the gas can. We had our backs to him at the time as we were reviewing the log where I had selected to shoot the perforations in the wellbore. We heard the explosion and saw him on fire. We immediately rushed to his aid by throwing dirt on him to put him out. Long story short, he survived to go on being a wise guy.

Jack was not very skilled in getting us solid projects, and I never wanted to do another project outside of Texas. However, as Jack was not a real oil and gas person (he was an MBA), he just wanted a deal he thought would sell. Not long after we moved our office to a nicer building in Los Colinas, Texas, we were fairly successful with funding the projects for the next year or so until the crew we had selling for us talked Jack into moving them into a very swank building in Los Colinas and separating from me. All of them were a bunch of know-it-all types with superiority complexes. They did develop a huge sales crew using my salesmen and my money to kick their new company off.

The crew never raised impressive amounts of money while they were in my office as they were getting their office expenses and health insurance paid by my company. But soon after they moved out of my office, two months later, they started raising $700,000 to 900,000 a month. It was obvious that they were holding back on their abilities to keep me from having a share in their success.

They were still expecting me to continue paying for their health insurance. It shocked Jack when I canceled their portion from my policy. I told him, "You want them to have insurance, then you pay for it."

He replied that he was on the policy as well. I said, "You're a big boy. Pay for your own insurance."

Jack's new crew had sales methods that were less than honorable, very underhanded, and unethical. I never would have allowed these guys to conduct business in that manner. This is more than likely why they moved on because Jack knew I would never tolerate such sales tactics. Later on, going through our bank records and canceled cheques, we noticed that Jack was using my company's checking account to pay some of his personal expenses and having his wife sign the checks, which I am sure was at his direction. After I discovered this, I canceled his access to my account.

They had the same acreage that I had in Illinois. Still, they had no clue about the proper drilling pattern. They started drilling an excessive number of wells on a quarter section of land, destroying the area's ability to be productive. Then I started looking in different areas to lease productive acreage for drilling. I had to get away from Jack and his new sales crew. He was using my marketing material and using some of my clients—one in particular, a very well-off individual, Dan. He had a PHD (parents had dealership) and did not have much sense, but he was a wise guy with much money.

Jack had his guys book him with the same project I presented him a couple of months earlier but used a slightly different book cover. This made the guy question me about my wells. I invited Dan to meet me in the field so I could prove that the wells belonged to my company. I waited three hours for this prima donna to fly in at a small airport. He came bebopping in on his private jet at a small Pike County, Illinois airfield. He got off his plane with not much of a greeting and absolutely no personality but straight away asked how far the wells were.

He wore an expensive plaid polo T-shirt, shorts, and ostrich-skin loafers with no socks. I used my typical Texas oil field humor and told him, "Gee, Dan, the ground thorns and cow shit will really mess your shoes up." I got no response in return. I recommended he rent a car at the airport and follow me and my pumper. After all, I did not want this knucklehead in the truck with me for five to six hours.

Not long after Jack's guys sent their deal to the PHD (Parents Had Dealership), this investor called and started busting my butt about the same deal being sent to him from another firm. I told him, "That is why I asked you to meet in the field to begin with." There was not any reconciliation with him. He just wanted to start a lawsuit and ruin me financially. I just wasn't the smooth con man Jack's new guys were.

Jack's crew continued marketing to my clients, which started another suit, and I told Jack that I was splitting from him and that there would be additional suits, beginning with a suit from myself as well as other clients. At that time, he did not believe me. I agreed with him that clients were not the property of any one company, but they were proprietary to my company in our instance. Everyone that was our client was being marketed by his new crew. I told Jack that this was an unethical move on his part and would most definitely start a war and class action lawsuits. Long story short, it did.

I told Jack that his crew would create more problems criminally for him and themselves, but he was so addicted to the pain medicine Dilaudid that he could not think straight and had convinced himself that I was the problem. Jack's new crew convinced him because they wanted me and my company to go by the wayside because they could manipulate their staff and convince the clients that my company wasn't raising enough money to accomplish the projects. He assumed that was why so many of our clients were suing us.

Jack thought I would be going to prison for what he thought was a white-collar crime and even told me he wanted me to be a good inmate. He was convinced of that because the attorney we were using on our mutual suits bailed out on me and convinced Jack I would be going to prison probably because he was one of those $1,800 per hour guys and he was smarter than any of us. He concluded that from all the lies Jack was feeding him about me, he knew better than any of us. Jack's crew were so full of themselves that they believed all the lies and felt they were untouchable.

These imbeciles were doing unconscionable sales tactics by using spare cell phones and passing themselves off as clients, giving fake names and absolutely false referrals for Jack's company. They were giving false reports about the success of their drilling programs (none of it was true). They lied about project field progress to their clients by exaggerating well production and reporting well completions that had not actually happened. All this was in the lawsuits against them not only from their clients but the FBI as well.

The FBI spent time in Jack's fancy offices, collecting data and shutting down his operations, and establishing their legal case; from what I understood, their case was airtight. They confiscated every computer and every paper file available. They did a raid on his office, and as nobody knew that the feds were on the way, they could not destroy any files.

Jerry and Chase, the leaders of the new team, had much arrogance. Chase recommended during a mediation to see who has the most money—them or us. He suggested paying them the $3,000,000 we were being sued for. But it turned out that the clients and the feds had more money. Of course, that would also include my company coming up with part of the settlement, but since none of the litigants were my clients, my only connection in the case was the projects they were suing over were on leases that my company paid for. I had nothing to do with the funds they sent to Jack's crew.

I declined to contribute any money to their suit; they simply included me because of guilt by association. I, unfortunately, knew Jack personally and his team. Jack had several shell companies, maybe eleven, and he more than likely moved money in and out of these companies. It didn't do him much good with the eds, though. The feds had them by their short and curlies with all the testimony given in depositions from their clients and employees, documents, and confiscated computers during court cases. There was not a chance that any of them were staying out of prison. And to the prison they went.

Most guys did five-year stretches while Jack had a ten-year sentence for white-collar crime. Of course, federal sentences are reduced by 15 percent, so none of them had to do the full time in lockup. On the other hand, Jack ended up with what would be a life sentence. After he had spent a little over four years in prison, he died from health complications from several of his health conditions. I guess the penal system took an immediate disdain for him because once he was in the medical unit and getting along fine with his health issues, they transferred him to the general population. They should have left well enough alone.

Jack's original cell was close to the infirmary, and he had access to medical care. When they moved him, about two months later, he started going septic, and they transferred him to a hospital for one day and then brought him back to prison that same day. The next morning, he was sent back to the hospital with the same condition. He later died that same afternoon. Jack never helped me much with my sales crew after he opened his new company with his star-bangled banner crew. We raised money for our projects, but it was nothing like Jack's new company, nothing like those superstars were doing with their lies and fake investor referrals.

Starting a New Crew

I went through a few guys before finding someone to help me in managing my sales staff. That is when I ended up with Mac and Carl. After two years of working with me, Mac and Carl decided to start their own company by once again taking my company's clients. It just goes to show that it doesn't matter to these guys if you are running out of money; they don't have any integrity about themselves or the contracts they signed. It's a theft fest of taking clients they have no right to as well as defaming me to clients and sales staff. As expected, these guys ended up doing their time out in federal lockup except for Mac, who died of self-inflicted lead poisoning from a .357.

Now, I have always cautioned people that if you want to start your own oil company, you may do it honestly. I would be glad to help you. Don't cheat me over as it always ends badly for guys that want to start their company at my expense; they usually end up in prison or pushing dirt from the bottom up.

These guys always want to begin with built-in clients and start with millions in investment dollars in hopes of enjoying immediate success. Well, such a success usually goes up their nose and leads them to Las Vegas.

I stayed out of the oil and gas business for a few months but couldn't get it out of my system. So I started another company in

August 2009 and selected a lease in View, Texas, as my first project to drill. It had three good locations to be drilled with the first drill site offsetting a well that produced over seventy-five thousand barrels of oil in an eight-year period.

I contacted an investor that wanted to invest and who wanted to be on the inside of the company. Being in a money crunch, I hesitantly let him be on the board of the company *despite* him not putting enough money in to be as high up in the company as he wanted to be. He thought that we just made money because we were an oil company. I schooled him on how a company like ours made money. Then he demanded to be on our bank accounts. That is when I kicked him out of the company. He had absolutely no clue how to be in the oil and gas business. He was a little guy in stature and thought that since he was a multimillionaire (little Hitler-type attitude), he felt he could push everybody around because his money entitled him.

Nevertheless, it took about three months to fund the project, and we spudded the well in mid-December 2009 and reached a total depth of 4,800 feet just after Christmas. Drilling was progressing nicely until about 300 feet from the Caddo Reef when it was discovered the rig had deviated over 8.5 degrees from vertical, but by Texas RRC rules, they were only allowed 6.0 degrees, thus missing the reef entirely. I had cautioned the rig crew to watch their ROP ("rate of penetration") at a certain depth because we felt we had a reef play at a certain depth. However, they absolutely blew right on by the zone; we ended up declaring a dry hole and plugging the well and abandoning the site.

We spent the next few months without a project to drill until March of 2010, when we came upon a Lease in Dewitt County, Texas, and created an Oil Income Project. The teams I had in Fort Worth, Texas. Came on board in early April 2010 and were hired to market the Oil Income Fund Project. They only had a month trying to place investment funds. However, that is when I suffered a massive heart attack in early May 2010 and spent thirty days in the hospital undergoing four surgeries with two of them being open-heart bypasses.

I spent the next three months recovering. Most of my time in the hospital was spent in the cardiac care unit. It took about another six weeks for me to start healing enough to be able to work a few hours every day. After all, I had major multiple open-heart bypass surgeries and coded twice in one day in the hospital. About an hour later, when Shaq, the PA for the heart surgeon, had removed the electrical leads in my heart, I felt a sensation that didn't seem right. All around my heart and incision, I felt a very warm sensation (I was bleeding internally from my bypass grafts). The last thing I remembered that day was Shaq doing chest compressions on top of me as I was being wheeled off for another open-heart surgery. Going to the office part-time, attempting to help market the Oil Income Fund Project, it became clear the guys I had hired there couldn't sell; so I shut that office down in the first part of August 2010 and moved back to the Dallas area.

After moving back to Dallas in September of 2010, we started having minor success with both raising money and good wells.

When I recovered enough from the heart surgery, I met with a fellow that I knew, Eddie, to help me with lease acquisitions. We found a lease containing over thirteen thousand acres in Pecos County, Texas, with existing production and plenty of reliable geologic data. While I was getting my study together on the thirteen thousand acres and getting backup geological data together that would be placed in our presentation material, which would be irrefutable, we needed another project to fund.

Not long after I shut the previous project down, Eddie and I found a location in Southeast Texas that had several exciting wells ready for the Rework/Return to Production Project and a deep disposal well that I had big plans for later. I brought several partners from past associations on the Rework/Return to Production Project. We sent the company we bought the lease from and were using as licensed operators for this lease more than $100,000 for the start of work to be performed. They told me they would start the work on the wells in the first week of January 2011 and begin workover procedures immediately. In the first week of February, I called the guy in charge of the workover procedure, who told me the rig broke down thirty miles from the location. Knowing that these old rigs broke down often, I let him slide on it.

The next call I placed to him was three weeks later, and the rig was still being repaired. I told him, "Don't piss on my leg and tell me it's raining." I instructed him to get a rig on location without any further delay and start the workover procedure they promised to be doing. But a few weeks later, no work was still being performed, and he told me they could start soon if we gave them another $80,000. It wasn't difficult to see what they had done with the money that we had invested previously.

The guy did get another rig on location, which happened to be the most expensive rig in the area, and did a block squeeze procedure that ran well over $60,000 and blew our budget out of proportion. While the procedure worked well, it ran our project over our planned cost. Since this was a turnkey project to the tank, we couldn't charge our partners for the overage. The guys had other field service companies they contracted with for our project that they didn't pay either. These guys also had not paid the Texas Railroad Commission their fees for allowing them to be bonded and licensed in the state for oil field operations. I eventually hired an attorney to get our funds back or get the lease turned over to us. As typical, the process with court took a stupid amount of time, two years to be exact, which we prevailed on. To say that attorney fees were absurd as well is an understatement. During this time, the well was producing, and we were spending money on field activities; we even increased the client's net revenue interest, foregoing any interest we could have been entitled to in the project taking so long to get to the income phase for their patience and didn't charge for court cost and attorney fees. All this proves no good deed goes unpunished; the clients showed no appreciation for my generosity and expected the increase in net revenue interest to be permanent.

We then purchased a location deep in South Texas so close to the Mexico border that I negotiated what I thought was a fair trade with the operator of record on the lease. This would be a site on which we would try out submersible pumps, and I included the cost of four pumps in my purchase price. I sent Ronald, the leaseholder,

$150,000 for the project and learned he couldn't honor the lease agreement working interest and net revenue. I demanded the total return of my investment; he returned $100,000, but he had already been through $50,000. We came to an agreement for him to act as operator of record on another location to balance out the remainder he owed me. Still, he was ridiculous to expect the rest. I told him to forget it and that I would refile my suit on him.

This location was so far south in Texas, and on my return home from this location, I took a different route home to avoid all the slow-moving Eagle Ford drill rig traffic; I headed west to Laredo, Texas, and then north on Highway 35. I had to go through a large border check station a few miles north of the border on Highway 35. As I pulled into a spot for the agents to check me and my truck, they got this scraggly-looking dog up. I told them, "Don't let your dog pee on my wheels."

They replied, "This is a drug-detecting dog."

I responded to them, "I am fresh out of drugs on this trip. You will have to get your own."

Turns out the border patrol guys didn't have a sense of humor. They then asked me if I was an American citizen. I responded, "What the hell do you think? I look like a redneck. I sound like a redneck, and I'm driving a lifted redneck-looking truck. Of course, I am an American citizen."

After my exchange with them, I believe they had their fill of me and waived on through. It reminded me of a golf buddy of mine, Frankie. He told me of the story when he was coming home from a very successful golf trip in California, where he had to go through a border patrol station, and they asked him if he was an American citizen. Of course, Frankie was of Hispanic descent and said, "Yes." They asked him. "Well, who is the president of the USA?"

He said, "Some actor…let me think…oh, John Wayne."

They replied, "Come with us."

Late in 2011, I hired an ISO ("independent sales office") out of Florida with Charles as the lead guy to do the marketing for our projects. After several conversations with Charles and some of his team, we came to an agreement, albeit not in writing, for his team to commence marketing efforts in November 2011. In the middle of December 2011, we developed the water disposal project; as portions of the disposal project were beginning to be received, we felt the best way to communicate with partners was a website where we could regularly update each project. The disposal project was a no-brainer where oil producers in the area paid to dispose of produced water with residual oil production.

The trade we stroked with the mineral owners was we only had to pay the 5¢ a barrel of water disposed of and 3 percent of any oil we recovered from the water we disposed of. It took the sales team until July 2012 to complete the funding.

This should have taken a month at best to fund; it had no drilling downside and all upside potential.

Before the disposal project, I had a sales team in Tulsa led by George selling a project that reentered four previously drilled wells. The wells had zones that were never produced from. The project was considered an EOR ("enhanced oil recovery"); we decided to do what's called radial jet drilling where a specialty company sends a cable tool down the hole and drills out latterly in several different directions where that procedure opens up several drain holes in multiple productive horizons. At the request of the specialty drilling company, we conducted a test on each well to verify that each well had a good cement bond so their procedure would work; all wells showed good cement bonds.

After a few months, the company decided the cement bond wasn't good enough and the procedure would not work. I did a bit more investigating on this company; we had already paid them $360,000, and they invoiced us for another $100,000 that I refused to pay. Their excuse was typical they used often, and several of their prior customers had complained of the same thing.

We produced over three hundred barrels of oil before a leak was discovered in one of the storage tanks. Not long after that, since it was clear the project wouldn't be productive, we sold the oil and shut it down. I sold the surface equipment, sent the partners their pro rata share of all proceeds from field sales, and sent their K-1 tax reports. Once again proving no good deed goes unpunished since the partners' funds had been expended in the field, I should have reimbursed my company for going over budget, deducting their pro rata share of their cost out of the proceeds from the sales after all the project was a turnkey working interest deal.

We bought the lease from an operating company that never spent a dime on the property except for fees to the state for being the operator of record, which transferred over to my company. When we listed ourselves as operators, we paid Larry, the owner of the other listed operating company, for the acreage and paid the Texas RRC for listing us as operators. Our signage for each well and the lease was a cost as well. Gil played a role in this lease a few years after I had already paid the partners their funds; he put his company lease sign on the lease and listed it as a 1,200-acre lease, which was nowhere close to that acreage. It was no more than 270 acres. How Gil felt entitled to the lease was beyond my comprehension.

He paid nothing to me for the lease; and Larry, the previously listed operator, colluded with Gil to transfer it.

I showed George that clients want all or nothing and myself being the guy in the white hat doing as much as I could for the partners and project, none of which did anything for client relations. They felt they were entitled to more than they deserved. One day I will learn the oil and gas business is not a business of favors. George was a good salesman and a good person; however, he thought he could run an oil company himself and keep all that was considered commission to himself. A few months later, he found that running an oil company wasn't that easy. It's an affliction most sales guys suffer from—believing they can do better, not charge the client as much for the project, and keep more profits. Most of the time, it never works.

I warned George that the oil and gas business is filled with stress and dishonest people; he should stick with me. Together we could do good things for the clients. I reminded him of the series of heart attacks I suffered starting in January 2000, then November 2007, and the big one in May 2010. All this was a result of business-related stress. He still felt he could do better. George, a member of the Latter-Day Saints, didn't believe in working on Sundays. I reminded him that oil and gas wells run on days that end in *y* and break on the same days. He didn't pay any attention to me and started his own oil and gas company and, maybe six months later, suffered a fatal heart attack himself.

I had already packaged a workover project with a "two new drills" program. The sales crew was ready to send sales brochures and quickly raise project funds. The workovers had good oil shows and started production immediately. The new drills had good "shows" in the first well; we offset a well that a major oil company drilled to 7,400 feet in 1975 and hit a shale zone.

Since nobody knew how to complete a shale zone in 1975, we were ahead of the curve since our new well was drilled and ready for completion in 2013. There was plenty of knowledge on shale completions during this time, and the well was completed successfully. The well started producing over 186 BOPD on a one-fourth choke. I used a consultant to oversee the drilling; this was my first deep well in this area, which was deemed a shallow-only field. I wanted to make sure it was going to be a good well.

The consultant's employee was on site when one of my clients drove there to see it and asked the field guy where the existing workover wells were located; the consultant's employee knew nothing about my project and didn't call me to advise me there was a partner on location. He told the partner there weren't any existing wells to be worked over. The next thing was that the client claimed fraud and wanted his money back. I obliged him and told him where the existing wells were located, and before he started acting like an ignoramus about a refund, to put a call into the consultant I used and had him explain the incident.

The client still wanted a refund. I told him he could kiss both sides of my ass and to sign a release document or no refund. Of course, he modified the release with all sorts of asinine clauses. I told him he could try again without any additions to my release, or he could screw himself on any refund.

The consultant was on location for the next well to be drilled. I told him about the problem his employee caused and had a bit of an attitude about it. I knew how to handle it with him, so I headed to the site trailer to calm down. While looking at the drilling monitor,

I noticed he was using an abnormal amount of wellbore conditioner, which made it impossible to get a good mud log. It also ran costs up with chemical expenses, and the mud engineer spent more time than necessary. We had a new mud logger on duty. She was a degreed geologist from UT, rather young, just graduated by two years, and truly knowledgeable; but the consultant thought he knew better.

Because he had been in the industry for many years, while experience does speak for something, it is supposed to be mixed with intelligence and practicable learning; he eventually ran her off with his arrogance. Not long after, I learned he was drinking heavily while on duty, so I had to get rid of him. It is a well-known fact alcohol, drugs, and drill rigs don't mix well.

The Consultant with No Conscience

I hired Gil, another drilling consultant, and we started getting excellent results. Some of the wells tested over 300 BOPD. We drilled the second well of the project and had tremendous success discovering a zone that had never been produced. We declared it a discovery well. I filed a field discovery with the Texas RRC, and we released a press release on it. We began completing the wells and building an enormous tank battery, ten 436-barrel oil storage, four 210-barrel water containment tanks, and four 800-barrel gun barrels set on a twelve-acre pad built from caliche. Not to mention all well sites and roads were constructed from caliche; the site looked like a major oil company that we all know is listed on the big stock exchange constructed the site. Gil built all this because he had an excavation company and several pieces of dirt-working equipment. These services were overcharged as well.

As we were staking locations for the next five well sites, Smokey, the landowner next to our state lease where we just drilled three successful wells, thought it would be funny to switch our staked locations on two planned drill sites. We didn't notice until we had started drilling on our #5 site. We reported this to the Texas RRC field inspector since the locations wouldn't match our GPS sites. As required by the TXRRC, all well locations, whether successful or not, must have exact locations identified. He did visit the landowner and made him aware that what he did could be considered a state jail felony. During drilling, we had several strong shows of yellow oil on the pits and, during testing, showed seventy-two barrels of oil per hour. This is why Smokey got so upset at our drilling on his property because he had no mineral rights. He was just a surface owner. The stupid SOB should not have bought acreage in a rattlesnake-infested scrubland.

Early in March 2013, while drilling and reworking existing wells in Pecos County, we tested the southeast lease site disposal well for casing integrity for potentially turning this well into our disposal site. Turned out that the well we planned to serve as a disposal well had several casing problems. I scratched the location and started to develop another more favorable site, or so I thought. We then purchased a location in the Giddings, Texas area and fourteen 436-barrel storage tanks with stairs and landing along with three 750-barrel gun barrels. We had paid for sandblasting inside and out on all tanks and for coating the inside with corrosion inhibitors; the tanks were also to be primed. When we sent the trucking company to the location of the tanks for transport, we discovered none of the work we had paid for had been performed, and the tanks were rusting and in no condition to be repaired. As a matter of fact, their only value was scrap metal. To boot, there were only nine tanks (one of them had collapsed), the stairs and landing weren't present, and none of the gun barrels were present.

Living proof, most of the guys in this business are nothing more than thieves. I sent this crook a demand letter for the return of all our money, including the lease cost; since we paid him for the lease, the lease we selected not only had failed casing, but the RRC had ordered the wellbore to be plugged six months before the purchase. The RRC only ordered my company to plug the well because we sent them our information for the transfer of operator of record, a typical move on their part since they don't make changes on their site until a lease transfers. The RRC has been extremely difficult to deal with for quite some time, especially with operators that aren't considered majors. Some years prior, the RRC was managed by technical people, engineers, geologists, and others with real-life field experience. They since have people in the office that appear to be staffed by nothing more than computer types.

I decided to move the disposal site to Pecos County since this location already had two injection wells and a twenty-acre pad site that we cleared and developed. We bought new tank battery storage and gun barrels along with all other associated equipment that I had previously purchased and found it was all junk. I was sure this site would be best for all partners and the project.

We also drilled a water well for freshwater sales since many drillers and transporters needed fresh water for wash-downs on their equipment. Several cementers needed this location for washing the equipment down, and drilling operations required fresh water for their tanks. Moving the disposal site to Pecos County seemed the natural course of progression since shale exploration and production grew faster here than in any other oil exploration area.

Our business plan would keep this site running nonstop daily for years. Our location for this was right on Road 1450, one of the most traveled oil rig roads in the immediate area. It appeared to be the most advantageous geologically and economically solid move for the project.

My company paid for all the work and equipment. We also paid for the lease three years prior and did the dirt work through Gil since he had an excavation company and equipment. We set him up with an ideal situation where he could have one of his employees manage the location, and Gil would get half the profits just for being at the right place at the right time. I guess half of the gains weren't good enough for him. He later claimed this lease belonged to his company, but how he determined all this was beyond me. I spent over $3,000,000 on this location, far more than we raised on the original disposal project, but the payoff would be five times what we initially projected. Gil was in charge of permitting the site for commercial disposal and assuring the injection well could accept formation water from the zones being produced from not only our wells but all wells in the entire area. Gil was also being paid to perform this work; he would receive income from the site. You might ask how did that work; the correct answer is *not too damn good*!

This whole time we were drilling wells on the leases we purchased several years ago in Pecos and having damn good success. We drilled seven more wells since our drilling campaign began in early 2013 and hit every well with only two being slightly marginal. This brought our total well count to eight new wells that we drilled, averaging $180,000 over budget on every well. We also bought acreage on Highway 10 east of Fort Stockton, Texas, about ten thousand acres with existing wells and several locations to drill deep wells. We started reentering some of the existing wells on the Highway 10 site. We replaced downhole equipment, refurbished the surface equipment, and found we needed to permit an injection well since the wells were making high volumes of formation water; we did submit plans for an injection well. So through Gil's buddy, a landman in Midland, Texas, we started the process of injection well permitting, notifying all producers surrounding us.

Gil was moving tank batteries and flowlines, rerouting roads, and replacing equipment on his own. His work was several hundred thousand dollars in cost without my permission. I jumped his ass about it, and he agreed to deduct much of the labor, which in the long run, he never did. We obtained the water disposal permit since my company was the only group around for the quarter-mile radius requirement, which sounds stupid. Still, we followed the RRC rules and regulations. The rework wells started producing a load of oil every month (210 barrels). This is where I started suspecting Gil of theft; the equipment and the installation of the equipment I paid for weren't on location, none of the pumpjacks we paid for were present, and they were heavy-frame 640-size jacks about 2 1/2 stories tall tough to miss seeing these big boys.

Throughout his adult life, he has been a habitual offender, consistently engaging in deceptive practices. He showed no regard for the fraudulent billing of equipment that was never purchased yet still received payments for it. Additionally, he would invoice for work that was never performed, further perpetuating his fraudulent activities.

It appears Gil's bad behavior started with his numerous felony convictions, from possessing a controlled substance to manufacturing the same. In addition to his federal tax liens that amounted to over $2,000,000, he also had a federal conviction for evading taxes on diesel fuel. He has been guilty of transporting oil in his water-hauling trucks while never being charged with the previous; his employees have been caught doing so. Some of these charges should be treated and prosecuted as criminal fraud. His $2,000,000 federal tax lien was shortly paid for after he came on board with my company doing drill site consulting and site construction.

The leases further north from Highway 10 were where I discovered Gil was sabotaging my company and me by talking the land surveyor into permitting the leases and wells in his newly formed company name. Of course, none of this was discovered until late 2014 when we were fracking the first wells we drilled just south of Grand Falls. Most of these wells had twelve zones, and a few had eighteen zones. The frack crew engineer calculated about 6,500,000 producible barrels of oil in each well. During drilling on these wells, the mud loggers noticed several large gas kicks, and there was live oil covering the pits yellow in color indicating an extremely high grade of oil. The amount of oil indicated the well's capability of producing large amounts of oil, exceeding our projections in our memorandums.

We reached a total depth on these wells of 10,000 to 11,000 feet, which was 2,500 in excess of what I agreed to drill. This field started life as a 1,800- to 2,100-foot field called the Yates Field. This zone showed up in every well we drilled in Pecos County. When I told people where I was drilling and how deep I was drilling, they couldn't believe it, referring to this area as a shallow field; they were shocked at our deep drilling success. We ran very expensive logs on these wells known as rock vision; the logs were a mix of quad combo open hole logs and our mud logs showing all productive zones. The log showed where to perforate the zones, the recommended number of perforations, and how many zones should be perforated.

One of the most impressive aspects of this log was that it predicted the volume of oil production known as OIP ("oil in place") by calculating oil per acre-foot and the wellbore spacing by the total depth of the well. The log was quite expensive, but it eliminated the necessity for another costly and unnecessary wellbore testing. The engineers from the well testing company have a lab in their facility that tested our well data, and the company is a firm traded on the stock exchange. The engineers made several impressive recommendations about our wells. These wells could produce 6,500,000 barrels of oil per well at the time, which was about $120 per barrel. It was no wonder Gil started working the sales staff and investors against me. He also put his company name on our leases and signs on our wells and leases. This showed that he was the leaseholder and operator of record on my leases and production. This was anything but true; he effectively stole these leases from my company. He ultimately paid for this later.

The Six Mile Creek Project was transferred to the Highway 10 site lease, where my company paid $65,000 for four leases. We immediately reentered two wells and began producing daily and continued with production enhancement procedures. We needed to permit an injection well since the wells were older and started making high volumes of formation water. We submitted plans for an injection well through a Midland, Texas, landman of "Surface Specialties." We were counting on Gil to assist the landman in getting the injection well permitted and adequately equipping the site for on-lease water disposal.

Three sales runs were made, two in late December 2013 and one in late March 2014. But it was in constant need of repair, so several thousand feet of production tubing and rods were purchased and replaced in these wells in addition to workover procedures on two other wells. Gil began performing dirt work, installing new tanks, flowline reconfiguration, and moving existing tanks at several hundred thousand dollars in cost.

Gil never hooked everything up like he was supposed to and was paid to do. The fieldwork performed and paid for, along with the lease purchase, has far exceeded the funds raised for the project, once again putting my company's budget in the hole.

For the rework portion of the State Lease Project, four wells on the rework lease were reworked (only one by contract was required). Over $360,000 was spent replacing rods, tubing, downhole pumps, and acidizing procedures. Pumpjacks, electric motors, and concrete pads (pumpjack blocks) were also purchased for the work over wells.

In addition, my company contracted with an independent geologist Ricky to draft and file abeyance letters for the TXRRC to show the commission that no wells were producing for years before my company purchased the lease and subsequent production of the wells. We paid well over $30,000 for the geological report.

More from The Consultant

While fracking the state lease location in 2014, we discovered that Gil, using our geological report, had the P-4 put in his company's name and moved all equipment purchased for the work over wells by my company to the Ox "A" Lease. Gil was paid through his company for the oil my company produced; however, no disposition of that sale was made to my company, its partners, or the royalty owners. Though it is hearsay, Charles questioned Gil regarding proper ownership of the Easton Lease belonging to Patrick's company. Gil replied, "The lease wasn't in good standing, and I obtained the lease from RS Properties."

The State Lease #1, the first well drilled for the State Lease Project, had several successful zones; and we sat on-site during the entire twenty-seven-day process. The well cost came in at over $1,500,000 complete to the tanks. The Ox B #1 well was the second well to be drilled, and I sat on this site for the entire nineteen days it took to drill and set casing. This well came in far over budget at approximately $1,200,000 to complete the tanks. Only $2,800,000 was raised for the project, so after spending $2,700,000 on new drills and over $300,000 for workover on the Easton Lease and paying the marketing team, all profit that should have been the company was spent on cost overruns. The drilling company I was using was a company that was featured in a television series several years ago. The rig crew bragged about how they could drill our wells round, straight, deep, and cheap in less than two weeks. However, nothing could have been further from the truth. Their drill pipe not being of American-grade steel was the main reason for their delay as the pipe couldn't take the stress drilling. My company's sub docs clearly state that "initial operations" do not include installing any production equipment or enhancement; in addition, only one zone will be attempted per wellbore by contract. However, after the consultant completed the Woodford Shale, Gil came in and shot other zones without informing me. I only later discovered this while we were freshwater fracking the well.

On the Pecos IX Project, State Lease #2 began drilling on May 31, 2013, and reached a total depth of 7,354 feet on June 17, 2013. The #2 well had several producible horizons and made a very good well (this well was fresh water fracked in late November of 2014, which this procedure will be discussed later on). State Lease #3 began drilling on June 19, 2013, reaching a total depth of 7,370 feet on June 29, 2013. The reentry well of this project had failed casing and wasn't successful, but both new drills exceeded $1,300,000 in cost each to the casing point. The reentry well was approximately $90,000 in cost, and I also sat on these locations during drilling. Completion procedures for the new drills began in late September 2013, and several sections in each well had productive horizons available. Gil had a history of doing whatever he felt like doing without my consultation or approval; as a result, the completion cost of the new drills was approximately $800,000 each, and his incompetent field activities may well have rendered the wellbores not as productive as they could be.

The Pecos X Project consists of the Ox B #3 well and the Ox B #4/6 well. The Ox B #3 well began drilling on July 6, 2013, and drilled to a depth of 7,387 feet, which was reached on July 17, 2013. During drilling, the mud loggers noticed several gas kicks and very nice yellow oil on the pits. This well also had several producible horizons, which made, according to Gil, "This well made a very nice producer, and during testing, it showed seventy-two barrels of pure yellow oil per hour." Due to leasing problems, we were never able to make any oil sales from this well. However, it has been reported to me that Gil did sell oil from this well. As it turns out, our leasing problems were because the guy I bought the lease from was salvaging and reselling the production equipment on the Ox Lease, rendering it incapable of producing. At that point, it was impossible to simply walk up, turn well on, and place the lease back into production as the original lease called for.

During the resolution agreement's closing, Gil claimed that he was producing the Ox Lease. We were later advised by Gil that Ox B #3 well developed an H^2S problem, which deemed it improbable to produce the well in that condition at the depth it was completed in. This well also had several shows. The cost of the casing point was approximately $1,200,000.

The Ox B #4/6 was spudded on November 13, 2013, and had several shows of yellow oil on the pits during drilling. We reached a total depth of 11,037 feet on December 19, 2013. We balloted the partners for permission to drill deeper at an approximate cost of $450,000, which severely exceeded the drill deeper cost.

This well is the first well that we ran a Rock Vision log-on. This well had a cost to the casing point of approximately $1,950,000. The Rock Vision Log technique proved to be quite a valuable tool as it married our Quad Combo Electric Logs with our mud log, then having it evaluated by the engineers that explained several details about the wellbores, including a column on the log called OIP (oil in place) The log was quite expensive, but eliminated the necessity for another expensive wellbore test. The engineers made several impressive recommendations on the wellbores that Rock Vision was run on, such as where to perforate a zone, how many feet to perforate, and how many shots per foot to shoot. Our deep wells had an average of 6,500,000 barrels of producible oil each, and this was using an average of a 10 percent recovery factor, where typically a 30 percent recovery factor is the norm in the industry. Completion procedures began on Ox B #3 in late January 2014. We shot several zones; again, Gil, acting on his own, perforated and acidized several zones when we were only responsible for one zone. The completion procedures being performed by Gil proved he didn't have the talent necessary to accomplish these procedures.

The completion procedures for Ox B #4/6 began approximately in the middle of February 2014. We shot several zones; again, Gil, acting on his own, acidized several zones when we were only responsible for one zone. It took until early September to get a size 640 heavy-frame pumpjack delivered and set on the well site. Shortly after this, the Trans Pecos region received a record rainfall amount of over thirty-three inches in three weeks, flooding the area until the middle of October 2014. The same applies to these wells as did the VIII project in that equipping and wellbore enhancement were to be paid separately by all W.I. owners to the extent of their individual interest ownership, none of which was reimbursed to my company.

During staking and the actual drilling, the Ox B #4/6 well and the Ox B #5/7 well it was discovered that Smokey (the landowner) changed the site stakes for the Ox B #4 well, the Ox B #5 Well, the Ox B #6 well, and the Ox B #7 well, thus the reason for naming Ox B #4/6 and Ox B #5/7. Smokey thought this would be amusing and a slap in our face since he got so upset with us staking a well seven hundred feet from his house; by law, we are allowed two hundred feet from any permanent structure. I later found out Gil thought it would be funny to stake a well less than fifty feet from the house and not actually use it as a real location. Smokey continued to be a thorn in the side of my company, continually making complaints to the TXRRC. We reported Smokey tampering with the well stakes to the Texas Railroad Commission after discovering his betrayal; the inspector for the commission reportedly advised Smokey that this was a state jail felony.

The Pecos XI Project moved in and rigged up for the Ox B #5/7 well on October 29, 2013. We reached a total depth of approximately 7,200 feet on November 13, 2013, and had several shows of oil on the pits during drilling and released the drilling rig due to faulty drill pipe and slow drilling, taking too long to get to the total depth. We used a different drilling rig for this location, and it seems that a drill pipe vendor made it through the 34 Midland area, supplying less than desirable grade of drill pipe to many of the rig companies. During testing, this well-made, very nice producer showed seventy-two barrels of pure yellow oil per hour.

Drilling began on Ox B #10 on December 18, 2013. At about 3,300 feet in on this well, we encountered a high-pressure saltwater zone that took seven days to get under control. I later suspected Gil of intentionally creating the blowout; we finally reached a total depth of 10,490 feet on January 20, 2014. This will also have several shows of oil during drilling and will make a nice well. The drilling rig for this site, as well as the next several locations, was owned by a personal friend of Gil. While it was rigging up, we were videoing the process as we did on every location. We did this for our website for update reasons showing our partners the progress we were making. The drilling company got upset at our video, claiming they thought we would use it in case they had an accident during their rig-up procedures. Evidently, they had an incident that happened some months before showing up for our project. Gil called me and said we had to stop the video and explained their reason for it. I told him to get them off my lease (of course, I used a more colorful vocabulary). I chose the "G-rated" version of the book. I later discovered why they felt we needed video proof of their carelessness: This rig could pull triples when tripping drill string out of the hole. While performing this procedure, the guy on the tubing boards didn't pull hard enough on one of the pipes, and the pipe split in two. As pieces came crashing down on the rig floor, a piece hit me in my hard hat before I made it completely into the doghouse.

The Highway 10 Site Project #1 consists of the Six Mile Draw B #1, a new well, and B #204, a reentry. The B #1 well was spudded on February 10, 2014, and reached a total depth of 11,219 feet on March 11, 2014. It had an excellent show in the Wolfbone at 10,910 feet with several other zones up-hole, approximately twenty-one productive horizons. The drill rig appears to be slower than previous, and of course, this is a personal friend of Gil's. This well went far over budget as the cost to casing point was over $2,100,000, dirt work, tanks, production equipment, well treatment, and other completion cost was $1,100,000.

Dirt work, equipment, flow lines, and other completion costs for the reentry were $400,000, including abeyance reports needed for the Texas Railroad Commission.

Gil went far over budget on excavation and dirt work on this lease, some of which was for one of the family member's hunting leases, all charged to my company without my knowledge; these charges were so exorbitant we could never catch up.

I met with the Odessa attorney that married one of the Highway 10 site landowner's daughters. The Odessa attorney represented the family concerning all oil and gas leases. On more than one occasion, meeting with the attorney to discuss surface damages, he indicated to me (on my last visit in December of 2014) that he did not trust Gil and seemed hesitant but willing to work with my company.

The attorney wanted $40,000 per location for land damages, caliche, and lease water even though we hadn't used any of his lease water. I told him that the majors were paying these charges for prime Midland County property and that we could pay half that. He seemed agreeable with this and indicated he and the family were going on vacation to Italy. However, we never heard back from him, so I can only surmise that, once again, Gil's sabotage of my company and slandering me to him would be the reason for him never getting back to me.

Roadwork and location preparation costs were approximately $150,000, also extremely exorbitant. Logging reports also ran roughly $180,000, and repair work was charged for new wells not yet operational. The Highway 10 Project #2 consisted of the Six Mile Draw E #2, and again it was the drill rig that showed up to drill after I had instructed Gil to get a different drilling company. We spudded the well on March 16, 2014, and reached the total depth of 10,832 feet on April 11, 2014. This well also had several horizons of bright yellow oil on the pits during drilling, and we called in the logging company to run the Rock Vision log. Costs to casing point were $1,900,000.

Completion costs, which ran approximately $1,300,000, were charged and paid for (including pumpjacks, tanks, and other equipment) to Gil and his companies, but work was not performed. Gil even told the Florida sales team that Patrick's company was paying these invoices. Still, he wasn't forwarding the payments to the vendors because he wanted to ruin Patrick and his company. The

Florida manager didn't have the common decency to inform me of Gil's treachery.

The Highway 10 Site Project #3 consists of the Six Mile Draw D #1, and Gil's excavation crew used dynamite to excavate the cellar for this drill site on April 20, 2014, making site preparation costs quite expensive. Gil had commented that Kelli's company was the responsible group authorized to use dynamite. Only after we started our suit against Gil did I understand why Kelli was the authorized company owner to purchase dynamite as it required an FFL to do so.

Gil was a convicted felon making him not eligible to buy explosives. The well was spudded on April 22, 2014, and the total depth of 8,905 feet was reached instead of 11,000 feet due to a driller error twisting off the drill string on the bottom, leaving several hundred thousand dollars' worth of equipment that wasn't retrievable. The total depth was reached on May 19, 2014. There were several impressive shows with blooming oil cuts in the samples at the mud logger trailer. Gil was instructed to get the drill rig off the location, and they took too long to reach the total depth of each well. Being one of his friends, the rig was not fired from the location as instructed. This well appeared to have gone to $1,900,000 to casing point with completion costs of approximately $2,200,000 charged and paid for. However, regrettably, Gil, in his customary "good ole boy" manner, has disregarded the fact that my company never received the completion equipment for this well. He had assured himself of favor while warning against any scrutiny as he intended to cause significant trouble or deceive in ways previously unimaginable.

Each wellbore was perforated and acidized, although my company was responsible for only one in each wellbore, and a total depth of 11,460 feet was reached on June 28, 2014. This well was drilled without our permission by Gil, instructing his buddy's rig to move in. My company gave permission to do site preparation only, which was Gil's responsibility. Again, we had several productive zones according to the Rock Vision log. The cost to casing point was $2,300,000, but only $3,500,000 was raised; and after paying the marketing staff, my company was left to foot the rest of the well cost. According to the log, this well had a very impressive Wolfbone show. Completion costs of $1,750,000 were charged and paid for but never performed. The Highway 10 Site #4 Project consists of the Six Mile Draw C #1 well, spudded on June 4, 2014.

The West I Project was a three-well project to be drilled to the Yates Formation at approximately 2,200 feet and cased with 8 3/8 production casing to allow for deepening the well later on in its life without the need for drilling with a slim hole drill bit. Five pad sites were built for the three wells on this project; all pad sites had full construction, including plastic-lined reserve pits, cellars, conductor pipe, rat hole, and mouse hole set on each, all invoiced and paid for by my company.

The Pecos XII and the Pecos XIV projects never existed; we started bank accounts in preparation for them but never started those projects.

The equity offering was formed to raise capital to combat the spiraling field expenses suffered by each project. It seemed the better each project did, the more charges Gil mounted on. This project consisted of large portions of my company's interest in each project and was the brainchild of Charles and Gil, neither of whom offered up any of their interest in the project. Only one small position was placed out of this project, and the partner sued to get his money back. The suit included Gil and his companies—Gil himself, me, and the investor who sued my company—and all this after we had the resolution agreement in place, making Gil the responsible party.

Gil agreed to make restitution to the investor and even made the statement at the resolution, signing that he would meet with the investor's attorney about paying the investor; however, he breached his last payment of $38,000.

Gil once again appeared to be sabotaging my company in the field with ridiculous statements to vendors concerning my company's nonpayment of invoices, intentionally going over budget on every aspect of each well, making decisions and never consulting me, not installing pumpjacks and all other necessary related production equipment that we paid for.

He also failed to provide my company proper documentation required for my company to make reports to the TXRRC. Although this is hearsay, he would tell vendors that my company owed his companies over $5,000,000 in past due invoices, which was false. I also believe there were under-the-table agreements with several vendors. Such appeared to be the case with his buddy, the landman of Surface Specialties, who charged my company well over $360,000 for landman services while never obtaining the leases they were instructed to accomplish.

Another instance is Nicole's conversation with a vendor that refurbished equipment on a tank sandblasting invoice of over $55,000. Gil destroyed the invoice in front of the company owner, instructing him to make a new invoice for the poly pipe. Again, with a water hauler, he asked the owner to invoice my company for several water hauling invoices that had nothing to do with my projects.

Since the last few wells were drilled on Ox property that JXP LLC claimed they owned executive rights to, we contend that Natural Resources is the owner of the executive rights, which was proved up through an Odessa title attorney. In the beginning, Natural Resources was willing to work with us; later, neither JXP nor Natural Resources were willing to work with us, especially since Gil was taking every opportunity he could to assault my company and me verbally. This well would not be completed until a lawsuit between my company and JXP was finalized.

JXP requested Gil to submit to a deposition in January 2015 as he was listed as the vice president of record. My company was not responsible for the deposition is another example of Gil's sabotage of my company as his entire deposition sounded like he was purposely making it impossible for my company to prevail in its claims against JXP.

Gil claimed his contact at Natural Resources (purportedly, by Gil, the VP of the Permian Basin for Natural Resources) would help my company obtain the Ox Lease (which he did not); he hired his landman buddy of Surface Specialties back in September of 2013 for which he did nothing to solidify any lease for my company yet charged us over $360,000.

The delays by Surface Specialties, Gil, and the mistakes by the drilling company have cost my company in excess of $4,000,000 for the two wells. There were many excessive charges from several vendors. Fracking of the state lease wells and the Ox B-7 well occurred in the first week of December 2014.

Gil made all the arrangements for every vendor for these procedures, including but not limited to frack tanks (there were ten tanks on each site), water hauling, acid treatments, frack trucks, frack stack valves, and ECT. Gil suggested we charge $600,000 for each well for the treatments. He even sent me an AFE via email as a backup to send to partners for our assessment invoice. As it turned out, $600,000 for the treatment wasn't far off the mark since the frack tanks were there for over forty-five days and loaded with frack water along with the other invoices we received. These treatments came close to $550,000 per well, which my company paid.

Gil contacted several partners in these wells, instructing them not to pay my company's invoice as he thought it absurd and should only be $40,000 for each well (the tanks alone were $40,000 per well). In a conversation I had with Charles, he exclaimed Gil said, "Can you believe what Patrick is charging for the frack jobs?"— another example of the sales crew and team leaders destroying my company as not one word was said to me about Gil's lies.

Enter a New Conspirator

In September 2013, Charles hired Chester to raise funds for my company's projects. Charles portrayed Chester as a top-notch money raiser with high morals, ethics, and integrity. This was not the case with Chester as I discovered very late in his employment with us; he couldn't close a door with the instructions on the back side, and the majority of income paid to him was from me closing sales for him and from the overrides from other marketing staff members.

Chester didn't have an ounce of integrity in his butt; as it turns out, Charles didn't possess a bit of integrity himself. Shortly after having Chester on a field visit, he started communicating with Gil and making several trips to Midland, staying with Gil at his house. Chester, being the coward he was, started working his way in with Gil; and the two conceived a plan to put my company out of business.

Chester, Mark, Charles, and Gil attended the NOLA Money Show with us at my expense. I found out later that Gil and the team were walking around the exhibit center promoting their first project that I prepared for Gil, even paying my graphic artist a $5,500 invoice for map drafting. Gil told me he would cut me in on every sale and all revenue from the wells; we discussed a 5 percent ORRI. My company prepaid the expenses for the team to be in New Orleans, even paying for Gil and Chester's wife to tag along. Chester wanted full commissions on partners that we derived from anyone from the show. I told him that wouldn't happen since my company spent so much on the event exceeding $90,000. He used that as an excuse for not raising any money from the show. I reminded him he wouldn't even be here at the NOLA Show except for my invite to him.

To further elaborate on designing Gil's marketing literature, Kelli made a statement to me that the mapping appeared to be worth no more than $500. This showed their absolute disrespect for my input on their project as it took over three hundred hours of design work from Pam and me to get their project into a format of sales-worthiness.

Jumping ahead a bit, we completed many wells on the Highway 10 site. More money was spent than raised on these projects, which meant I had a truckload of my money in all these wells. At this time, Gil had everyone so twisted at me that no matter what I said, nothing would make a difference to any of the clients or staff members. In particular, there was a husband-and-wife sales team in Florida that I was extremely generous and good to, but they didn't give me any heads up as to Gil's treachery. The cost overruns were so bad the marketing team was told that invoices weren't being paid, which was an absolute lie. It created such animosity between the marketing team and myself that they quit selling my deals and started selling Gil's projects, which was not made apparent until much later.

At the NOLA Show, we showed our current investment project, and I paid for their wives to come along, all told—the floor space at the show, hotel, restaurants, and a door prize of a complete set of Callaway golf clubs and stand bag. I paid for the NOLA Show, all told; it set me back over $90,000. We saw one of our clients at the convention who commented we had such a nice booth and presentation we should have raised at least $3,000,000. It's hard to believe we didn't raise a dime.

I even had a fellow from Austin ready to invest with me but backed out at the last minute. I later found out Gil was going through the halls, passing his new company business cards out, and talking with people that had stopped by our booth promoting his deal and new company, which I helped him put together. None of my staff warned me about this scumbag and what he was pulling. We discovered that Gil had gone so far over budget with false invoicing, double charging, and many other areas of absolutely incompetent field activities, at least not until very late in the stage of this treachery. I could never catch up unless I started selling off some of my interest in the projects, which I ended up doing with the Equity Project.

Gil informed me that the attorney for the family of the ranch we were drilling on the Highway 10 site wanted land damages for our drilling locations. He indicated that he was familiar with the attorney and even friendly with him. Turns out the attorney had married one of the daughters of the original ranch owners. As usual, everybody had their hand stuck out since all oil companies were ultra-rich and had money to throw away. It made no difference to these self-important, pompous jerks that I was an engineer and spent weeks on end away from my family, three to four weeks at a time, on every drill site monitoring the drilling progress.

I met with the attorney, and he wanted $40,000 for each of our locations. I told him that the fee was the same as what ranches around Midland were earning from the majors drilling horizontal wells. Since we weren't drilling horizontal wells and were far from those majors' financial capabilities, I thought $25,000 was a reasonable fee, especially since they would be getting 20 percent of everything coming out of the ground. He seemed amiable to my offer. However, the family was going on vacation out of the country and said he would get back to me in two weeks. I never heard back from him.

I would just imagine that Gil had something to do with the attorney avoiding me. I even paid for dirt work on his ranch to improve roads for his hunting operation at no cost to him or his family. I paid over $80,000 to Gil and his company for dirt work improvements, cutting in new roads, who showed no appreciation or acknowledgment of my contribution.

Our drill times slowed. I told Gil to fire the drill rig company and not allow them back. But they were buddies, so this crew kept coming in. I gave them a time limit to accomplish the drill times, after which the drilling speed picked up.

The location we drilled next was a tough location to excavate. It took three weeks to level and create the pad and pits. The worst part of it was we had to use dynamite to get the cellar ready for drilling. I later learned that Gil's wife's company was responsible and charged for the dynamiting. The process required an FFL ("federal firearms license"). This is a license that an individual has to clear background checks for and be clear of any federal charges and convictions, something Gil couldn't accomplish since he had so many federal convictions racked up long before I ever met him. This well had several impressive shows with many of the shows having blooming yellow oil cuts in the samples. During testing, before we had even treated the well, it had 1,500 pounds of wellhead pressure, which was quite impressive since it only had been perforated.

The mud log showed several hundred feet of potential oil reserves, which later was proven with open hole logs and open flow testing; it tested at four hundred barrels of oil in a thirty-minute test. However, it seemed the better my wells did, the more Gil intentionally went over budget and slandered me. These wells started costing over $2,000,000 to the casing point each, which was over 30 percent of the actual cost. In short, some of the shenanigans going on appeared to be Gil getting under-the-table payoffs with more than the necessary cost of equipment.

I started suits with several companies; they started backing off their invoices and slanderous statements. To further elaborate on my suspected sabotage by Gil, he told several companies that I owed his company and his wife's company for overdue invoices totaling more than $5,000,000, which was an absolute lie. I paid for the flow line, tank batteries, pumpjacks, and other miscellaneous equipment, which he never delivered and never hooked anything up.

Gil also failed to provide my company with the requisite documentation required to file with Texas RRC. Needless to say, that put my company in a violation situation with the RRC.

To further explain why Gil couldn't use dynamite for his company, convicted felons can't have anything in their possession that requires an FFL clearance. Beginning in October of 1989, he had a conviction for drugs. I believe the conviction case type was listed as

Department of Correction. In March of 1990, he was convicted of marijuana possession; in August of 1991, he was convicted of larceny; in April of 1999, another Department of Correction for delivery of cocaine; in November 2000, possession of cocaine; in July of 2005, he had another Department of Correction. I believe this was where Gil was charged with manufacture with the intent of delivery. And finally, in March of 2011, he was convicted of motor fuel tax evasion. This dirtbag spent more time in prison than he did in oil field management. The information my attorney discovered on him would have been beneficial before I put him on our leases or introduced him to any of the staff or clients.

It gets worse.

One of my key employees had a conversation with Bill from an equipment refurb company that had an invoice exceeding $55,000. Bill told my employee that Gil tore the invoice up in front of him and said to make a new invoice out for poly pipe. Another instance was with a company that owned a water hauling company. Gil told the company to invoice my company for several loads of water hauling that had nothing to do with my leases. The next few wells we drilled were on a property where we needed help proving our executive rights. I hired a title attorney from Odessa that proved that I shared executive rights with a major oil company in Midland and that the landman we started with several months ago could negotiate with the major.

In the beginning, the other company was willing to work with us. Gil knew the other company quite well and took every opportunity to assault me verbally and my company. Needless to say, we lost out on this lease as well. I filed suit against the other company and subpoenaed Gil.

Gil's deposition clearly showed that he was ensuring I wouldn't win. After completing one of our wells on Highway 10, Gil suggested holding a group meeting in his Midland office to showcase our success to my sales crew. Everybody showed up, and we tested the well on Highway 10. That was so strong that all in attendance were very impressed. We showed them the rest of the lease, which was just as impressive. Although not immediately evident, Gil had already been defaming me to my marketing team.

The team was commenting that the partners are becoming intolerant with the field delays approaching. Though most knew Gil was my company's project manager, none understood or would have believed he was the prime reason for the slow time frames. Gil wasn't following my orders concerning well completions and scheduling. All our pumpjacks were the big heavy-frame #640 Lufkins and were painted the same, and the tank batteries all matched; the pad sites and roads looked like a major oil company put it all together.

Gil had suggested sometime in late 2013 that we let him communicate with our partners to calm them down. At the time, this sounded like a good idea, which appeared to work briefly. However, complaints from partners once again arose as, unbeknownst to me, Gil was delaying well completions and recalling oil pickups from our oil purchaser to hide his theft of our oil and sabotage us with slow revenue runs. After the staff meeting in Midland in June 2014, sales all but ceased as Gil had recruited the marketing staff away at the meeting as he was putting his company in place and had already formed it with the Texas State Comptroller. Alternatively, I was unaware of any disloyalty from anyone because no word was mentioned to me from our staff of Gil's treachery.

It was shortly after the June meeting I decided to start an in-house marketing crew for our Plano, Texas, office. Late in September 2014, we contracted with David and Tim to join my company as our in-house team. However, neither turned out to be very effective as they went until mid-December, only able to raise just shy of $150,000. Both were paid a $750 weekly draw and a 25 percent bonus on any funds brought in as well as receiving a contact list to call potential partners.

David, along with his weekly pay and bonus pay, averaged around 53 percent of the funds raised while Tim averaged approximately 27 percent. I told them they were welcome to stick around and continue calling, we would still provide office support, use of our phones with the contact list provided, and the best projects any company could offer; but the draws were over with since neither had any intention of repaying their respective draws. Both decided to move on to another company as neither had the nerve or talent to go straight for bonus pay.

Gil had already attended a trade show at which Jim had purchased a tiny area in the convention hall in Las Vegas in early February 2014; according to Gil, Jim had done such a lousy job that having my company's name linked with it was an embarrassment. Both Gil and Charles talked with me in mid-February 2014 about attending the trade show in New Orleans in October 2014. I had already decided to purchase booth space, and Jim's incompetence convinced me of the need for my company to make a proper showing in New Orleans. The show expenses included lodging, airfare, space rental, handouts, a set of giveaway Callaway golf clubs with a Callaway stand bag that I paid for my company logo to be embroidered on, and all materials including but certainly not limited to the current offering memorandum, the cost over $90,000. Not one partner was brought in by the staff we took to the show. Gil and Charles used this opportunity to further promote Gil's company and its first project that I helped Gil put together, paying $5,500 for map design.

I also paid the graphic artist to do his logo on the maps, the sales brochure, and other incidental items related to the brochure design. Gil assured me I was going to be reimbursed for our expenses, and we would be included in overrides from sales as well as a 5 percent O.R.R.I. in production, none of which occurred. In conversations I had with another sales guy, he indicated that Gil made claims that more than $3,000,000 was raised for his project from the NOLA trade show.

In March 2014, Charles met with an investor and his wife on the first project site south of Grand Falls, Texas. We had rig activity on this site at the time. The investor and his wife were well impressed with what we had accomplished. Charles took them to the Highway 10 site. This was even more impressive to them since we were drilling a deep well at the time. Both verbalized how excited they were to be doing business with my company and had the utmost trust and confidence in myself and the company. They also wanted to continue placing investment dollars with me and wanted to be counted in the next project. Charles and Gil met with the investors on the state lease site the next day where, most likely, Gil started working his way in on my clients.

More Turncoats

From this point, Gil started communicating with partners and obtaining their contact information through the marketing staff. Meanwhile, we were conducting weekly update calls with the marketing staff for several weeks. Fundraising from this point steadily declined. Gil suggested we hold a staff meeting in Midland at his offices in June 2014 so all in attendance could witness field activities. My company even paid for the entire trip costing over $27,000 (except for travel expenses for the staff). Although not immediately evident, Gil had been slandering me to the marketing staff and, most likely, to the partners as most were becoming intolerant of field delays by this time. Though most knew Gil was my company's project manager, none understood or would have believed he was the prime reason for slow time frames by not following my orders concerning well completions.

Later in December 2014, we began fracking the wells in Pecos County. These wells were close to Grand Falls, Texas, where we were fracking the first three wells we drilled. Each location had ten frack tanks full of water. We set each well site with a frack stack that was a multistage configuration. Also, we had a light tower at each location and another tank with chemicals on each site. The cost was over $550,000 at each location. When I asked Gil how I should invoice the partners, he recommended we price it at around $600,000 because I never priced it in their projects.

Gil sent an invoice form via email with his corporate logo that proved he created it. He even had it filled out with over $636,000 for each location for me to send to my partners. He later contacted my partners after I had sent our invoices out, and Gil recommended they not pay because it could be done for $40,000. My company had paid for the services, and Gil knew it because the charges came from his company. Much of the Frack bills came from his company.

Frack tanks at that time cost over $120 daily. Simple math works out to be $36,000 for the tanks. How Gil felt $40,000 would cover the entire cost of the frack job is beyond me.

While Chester was visiting Gil in Midland, they began scheming to get me out of the way. It started with getting the team leaders to the field for their dog and pony show. They bragged about field accomplishments like they were developing and creating the well placements. Far from the truth, I selected every well location, and I am proud to say I hit every well with only two wells coming up mediocre. Gil had the rest of the sales crew on location to showcase our wells. He also took them to his leases to show them the area he was starting his company with. Of course, no one told me about his betrayal, and he obviously told everyone to keep quiet about all of this until he had his leases purchased.

Gil approached me concerning placing him in charge as joint venture manager and operator of record since his intentional mismanagement was causing me a lot of problems with the partners. We had several conversations about this and solidified the decision while we were fracking the wells to go forward with the transfer; I did make it clear I had no intentions of being cut out of receiving revenues.

As negotiations continued about the decision for Gil to take over, he decided he wanted an attorney familiar with such transactions and SEC matters; that is where it started going downhill. The attorney he got was an insolent California individual that wasn't competent enough to take on anything related to oil and gas operations. I called off all negotiations since my local attorney, Billy, quit communicating with the California lunatic. As it turns out, that was probably the best thing to do. The California attorney called Billy way too often, and I wasn't sure Billy was the one to fight this for me.

Gil convinced five of my largest investors to bring a class action suit against me. More than likely, his California attorney had a hand in that; they charged me with fraud. I had no clue where the fraud came in because I drilled all the wells, hit each of them, and spent my money on completing them. Of course, that always seems to be the claim, so if their civil claim doesn't work, they always report to the feds so they can destroy a company.

I should have been insistent on defending the fraud claim and their other frivolous, unfounded statements. The most difficult of allegations to prove in court is fraud, which requires the accused to have malicious intentions and theft of part or all of the investment funds. Gil and his legal representation used all this litigation as an extortion attempt to get me to agree with the resolution agreement that Gil, his legal team, and five partners sent me.

Of course, my legal team was charging a combined $2,600 per hour, but they didn't possess one testicle among them. They should have challenged Gil and their clients with the fraud claims. I told my legal team this was the poorest excuse for representation and negotiations I had ever seen.

Gil approached me at the NOLA Show concerning putting him in place as joint venture manager and using his Texas operator's license under his wife's company as operator of record. This was further discussed in several conversations with him after returning from New Orleans. While we were fracking wells in December 2014 in the presence of Pam, Nicole, Charles, and Bill (another sales guy), it was decided that we would go forward with this decision. In January 2015, when Gil came to Fort Worth for a deposition, we confirmed with each other that we would go forward with the joint venture manager/operator change. After reading his deposition, it was clear he was not a team player.

As negotiations continued about his taking my company projects and the clients, his California attorney Larry made many attempts to put together the most one-sided contract favoring Gil. I then called all negotiations off as my then-attorney Billy was not communicating with Gil's attorney making my company look like idiots.

I then turned to the downtown Dallas attorney firm for legal assistance. Gil had convinced his "Dream Team" investor group of five investors to bring litigation against me and my company for fraud. I should have been smart enough to challenge the fraud portion and some of their other frivolous allegations in the suit regarding fraud and their other unfounded statements.

The most difficult of allegations to prove in court is fraud; and since fraud has to have malicious intent, with all the project wells drilled and completed along with production equipment installed, there was no fraud. This would have been impossible to prove since there wasn't any fraud, and no malice was presented.

The litigation directed against both myself and my company was strategically employed as leverage to compel me into executing a resolution agreement that would satisfy the opposing party. From my perspective, this coercive tactic can be considered a form of extortion. Of course, my legal team didn't possess one testicle amongst them to challenge any of my protests against Gil and his legal team.

Over the next several months, we continued negotiating with his California attorney making very little progress except to run legal bills close to $200,000. We finally came to an agreement that Gil managed to start renegotiating during the closing. It was at this point I told him there was no more room and he needed to pay my legal bill due to his attorney wasting time. He agreed to pay $50,000 plus our fee agreement on the sales price of the projects. However, my legal team talked me into turning over all project assets, including the money left in the accounts and oil in the state lease tank battery. All this amounted to over $426,000.

I told my legal team this was one of the poorest excuses for negotiating I had ever seen; but at that point, I was tired of being lied about, lied to, and being pursued by the so-called Dream Team for their frivolous crap. I was just ready to move on with life.

As Fracking and Stealing Continues

The State Lease #1 well, State Lease #3 well, and the B #5/7 well were fracked on approximately December 4, 2014. More than fifty thousand barrels of treatment fluid were used on each wellbore and even more on the B #5/7 wellbore, making it impossible to produce oil immediately. All three wells produced nothing but water for more than four months. The cost to haul water in for fracking was astronomical, and the cost to haul production water off the location to a disposal site was also astronomical.

Our half ownership of Gil's disposal site was supposed to cut costs on things of this nature. Still, he charged us for using our disposal site at a rate twice the going rate that Krystal paid without consulting me. He then hauled production water to the B-10 reserve pits, which was illegal and should never have happened. The pits were supposed to be drying so they could be covered up. This action caused us additional costs to empty pits, and we were later cited with a violation by the Texas Railroad Commission. Gil also charged us with hauling water and water disposal, which he did not do.

Ten frack tanks in each location held approximately five hundred barrels of water each. Frack tank rental for our procedures was

$120 per day for each tank, and Gil ordered them delivered far in advance of being needed. Eventually, they stayed at each location for about sixty days. Two acid pump trucks for each location were required; we were also required to pay their diesel cost exceeding $10,000 for each frack.

There was also a frack engineering truck and crew on each location that exceeded $15,000 per frack; light towers were rented for each location at the cost of $550 per day and were there for at least six weeks. Frack valve rental was approximately $27,500 per location and Gil's consulting fee of $1,250 per day for sixty days. Gil told all of our partners not to pay their frack bill because he could do it cheaper, but he was the one that ordered the equipment and associated incidentals that caused our costs to exceed what we had charged for the frack job.

Gil was also the one that advised us on what to charge the partners for the frack job. And he sent us an AFE to reflect those charges.

Prior to the implementation of fracking, we had suspicions for a period of one to two months that Gil had been redirecting the oil purchase trucks, and these suspicions were later confirmed when our employees responsible for oil purchasing validated these occurrences. Also, Gil was managing the field activities in a way that would hold production down. My company was led to believe that it was due to the wells needing rework and electricity issues.

After fracking in December 2014, I learned Gil was turning oil purchase trucks away. I verified that by contacting our oil purchaser, and they verified that Gil had been turning oil trucks away for four months or so and reporting to me that we had electrical issues. He had even filed false invoices relating to power issues and repairing them.

I told Gil that I was coming to Midland with my wife, and he indicated that he and the family were going to be traveling to Southlake, Texas, to attend his sister's funeral. I told my assistant at my office about that, and she sent them flowers. Pam and I traveled to the well sites and found no electrical issues with any of our locations, and there was no proof any repair had been performed. With that evidence, I traveled to Gil's office in Midland and told him to reverse the invoices he sent for electrical repair since I knew he was lying. The flowers she sent were on his desk, and when his daughter came in later, she inquired what the flowers were for and who sent them. When he told her they were for his sister's funeral, she gave one of those whiskey-tango-foxtrot looks. I knew then he was an absolute dirtbag liar. I have always believed a family death is nothing to use as an excuse, and his sister died probably four years earlier. This would later on come up to bite him in the butt. As his son was killed riding a four-wheeler on the back lot of his equipment yard leading onto a well-traveled road running into an oil field truck, I was truly sorry to hear of this.

It was later discovered in March 2015 that Gil was using his water trucks to pick up oil from the state lease and lease bordering tank batteries and disposing of the oil in some other manner. I had a fellow who was familiar with oil and gas travel with me to the field in March of 2015 where we witnessed one of Gil's water trucks taking fluid from the load line (oil pickup line) at the state lease battery and then drive to the bordering lease battery and do the same thing; this fluid could only be oil.

I verified this with a visit to my site with an associate that had nothing to do with my company. We witnessed one of Gil's trucks taking fluid from the load line (oil pickup line) at my tank battery and then driving to another tank battery and doing the same. The truck driver indicated he was taking water out of the tank. I told him he was a liar because he was hooked into the load line, not the lower valve, which was the water line. I escorted him off my lease and advised him not to come back.

I sent Gil a letter of dismissal of pumper duties. It appeared that he had no intention of leaving my lease since he was making too much money stealing from me. Later on, Gil had another one of his drivers attempt the same thing. At that time, my new pumper was on duty and could call the local deputy. He was made to load the oil back into the storage tank. The local deputy told me all this was a civil matter, and I told him he was spineless. We later contacted the Texas Rangers and reported the attempted theft as we felt they were the proper authority to report all oil field theft to. It turned out they were spineless as well. We reported this to the Texas RRC since water haulers aren't licensed and permitted to haul oil. We also reported it to the Texas General Land Office. Since this lease was on state lands, the theft affected them as well.

On March 23, 2015, my company sent Gil a release letter dismissing him of his duties as a pumper for all my projects. This letter was disregarded as his California attorney had been in communication with our staff and clients. Gil felt no obligation to abide by the dismissal. In April 2015, our newly designated field person stopped one of Gil's water-hauling trucks connected to the load line (the line used for oil transportation). The tanker was full of oil, and the county sheriff was summoned to the location.

A police report was made, and the Texas Railroad Commission and the Texas General Land Office were notified.

As the state is the owner of the minerals on the state lease, it is entitled to receive revenues from all oil extracted from the lease. Consequently, the theft not only affected us but also deprived the state of its rightful share of the proceeds.

Gil's sabotage apparently began in late 2013 when he started communicating with my marketing team, and it escalated when he started obtaining client contacts from the team leaders. Of course, I knew nothing of this dirtbag's treachery until early 2015 when we were going back and forth on our agreement to have him as JV manager and operator of record. He was sabotaging me and my company by defaming me with my team and the clients.

As usual, it seems people only want to believe negative statements. I felt like an absolute fool for going overboard on well sites and protecting the team; no good deed goes unpunished. I sent Gil a noncircumvention and nondisclosure agreement since he was obviously taking every advantage to ruin me. His California attorney told him not to sign since he never worked for me. I asked him what difference that made; not being an employee should have nothing to do with it. The no-good answer came from him, but I told him I could only surmise he was already violating the NCND Agreement and told his California lunatic attorney to study up on Texas employment laws. He then sent me an agreement drafted by his attorney, but it was so one-sided in Gil's favor that I refused to sign.

I also believe Gil's California attorney was involved in conference calls with my clients and team leaders in late December 2014 after I fracked the wells. Gil even had one of his employees pretend to be an investor calling my clients to give weekly updates, which was nonsense.

I felt all this represented fraud and collusion with his attorney planning and encouraging his moves. It also represented torturous interference with business practices. I wanted my legal team to charge Gil and his attorney, but that required them to have some guts.

In January 2015, when Gil was in Dallas, Texas, for his deposition with JXP, he suggested that he could take over all of our projects, leases, partners, and vendors. He would, in essence, become the Managing Venturer and operator of record for the TXRRC. Gil first made this suggestion at the NOLA Money Trade Show that my company paid for in October of 2014 where he indicated that my company would retain their working interest; later, he negotiated that out of the picture from my overpaid, weak legal team.

As Negotiations Begin

In February 2015, we provided Gil with a noncircumvention and nondisclosure agreement, but he chose not to sign it based on the advice of his attorney, Larry. We then offered him another agreement to modify the joint venture management, but once again, he refused to sign it under Larry's guidance.

In early March of the same year, Gil sent us an agreement drafted by Larry, which heavily favored his interests and placed all the responsibilities on us without any compensation. This agreement was clearly unjust and impossible for us to accept. During the negotiation process, Gil and his attorney conducted conference calls with our clients and marketing team leaders, possibly starting as early as December 2014 after we completed the well fracking. Furthermore, Gil's employee, Len, pretended to be a client and provided fraudulent weekly progress reports through robo-update calls, which I considered deceitful.

At this time, we hired a downtown Dallas law firm to help with negotiations and write the agreement for us. I informed them of the weekly calls being conducted to defame me and my company, but they lacked the nerve and integrity needed to defend us even though their average hourly rate was over $2,600.

Negotiations continued for another three months as Gil's attorney was extremely combative, calling my legal team daily; the legal cost ran to over $200,000. I finally told my team not to accept any further calls; the terms of the deal were presented, and they could take or leave it. At this point, I went with the adage that no deal was better than a bad deal and made Gil pay for his attorney, running my legal team's bill up.

Gil's sabotage and treachery forced my wife and I to move from a very nice home on Lake Granbury and sell our Cadillac CTS-V, Skeeter bass boat, and several other personal possessions just to survive. I later learned Gil lied about our financial ability to the clients, stating we had several hundred thousand dollars in jewelry, and the lake home was bought with investor money (it wasn't). It was a leased home that we had to vacate several months early and were sued for the remainder of the rent. He also accused me of having over $10,000,000 in overseas money, all of which was absolute idiocy. He was an excellent con man.

As a requirement of Gil signing the resolution agreement, he was required to pay all outstanding debt he escalated uncontrollably by false invoicing, under-the-table payments to him, and overbilling. All of this was invoiced for work that was never performed. He was also responsible for communicating honestly to the clients and sending out revenue payments; he did send out revenue payments. However, the checks he sent were minuscule in value, and all of them were NSF.

The clients began calling me in an attempt to collect from me for bad checks that Gill wrote. I informed everyone who contacted me that they had previously voted to remove me from JV management and operator of record, clarifying it was not my company responsible for sending the checks. I emphasized the importance of using their own judgment and taking appropriate action by contacting the district attorney for Midland County to report Gil and his company for issuing fraudulent checks.

Moreover, and as mentioned previously, Gil's thievery, sabotaging my company, and conspiring with our clients and staff caused us irreparable harm, forcing us to move from the home in Granbury,

Texas, to a cheaper home in Fairview, Texas. Additionally, I was compelled to sell my Cadillac CTS-V at a quick sale, incurring a loss of $30,000. Furthermore, we had to sell our Skeeter boat at a quick sale, resulting in a loss of $20,000. The monies we derived from the sale of personal assets were used to fund the office to the extent we realized we were fighting an uphill battle and had to throw in the towel.

Gil wanted two years to pay all outstanding debts. I replied that it was his duty to negotiate with all vendors. Unbeknownst to me, he never intended to perform the responsibilities he had agreed to. I know this was coming back to bite me square in the ass. Not long after signing the resolution agreement, several lawsuits, judgments, liens, and bank account garnishments ensued on my company. It was evident that Gil was conducting business in his usual manner with no intentions of being honorable.

Gil had a clause in the agreement that allowed him to appoint an attorney to defend my company and hold us harmless and blameless from any lawsuits, whether they are pending or future. This attorney was directed by my agreement with Gil that anything pertaining to Gil's company be directed to Gil and be his responsibility. This didn't turn out as agreed to. It was obviously a purposeful collusion between Gil and his attorney to deflect any responsibility of Gil onto me. Also, as our contract called for, his attorney never joined Gil or any of his companies as third-party responsibility as the indemnifying company.

Meet the Slimy Attorney

Gil's attorney agreed to several judgments against my company, never notifying me of any of the details and allowing one of the companies to garnish our bank account, costing me over $30,000. All of this was in direct conflict with our resolution agreement. We also suffered additional legal costs since we had to appoint a different attorney to defend us.

Gil's attorney also failed to appear in several suits that I wasn't aware of, earning us several default fees in judgments, proving that he was extremely unethical. When speaking with him, which I only spoke to him on one occasion, I thought he was an arrogant jerk. He ignored a deadline for a lawsuit response to an opposing counsel, which earned him a sanction from the court.

The attorney was so arrogant and dishonorable in representing my company that I was compelled to file charges against him with the Texas State Bar. He was sanctioned by the bar but not penalized anywhere near enough. Since it was apparent that Gil had no intention of honoring our resolution agreement, I initiated a lawsuit against him, charging him with breach of contract, defamation, slander, liability, common-law fraud, and statutory fraud. The suit also called for a complete rescission of the resolution agreement.

My legal team filed for receivership since this is the only way such a vile reprehensible person like Gil could be controlled and forced to comply with the provisions of the resolution agreement. He accused me of forging his name on Texas RRC paperwork that rescinded his ownership and ability to act as Operator of Records. He signed the paperwork in front of my legal team and several of his representatives. Gil was so incensed that I would exercise my right to reversion of the agreement that he conjured as many lies as he could think of to obstruct me from my rights. A week before a court hearing, he had sent an email to us and even left me ridiculous voicemails making threats in hopes that blackmail and extortion attempts would motivate me to drop our suit against him.

Since Gil's lack of sincerity in honoring the resolution agreement became clear, my company initiated a lawsuit against him and his companies in Dallas County. As stated previously, we charged him with breach of contract, defamation, slander, common law fraud, and statutory fraud. The lawsuit also called for receivership since this was the only possible way to handle a case with a neutral field operation company.

Gil is such a vile, reprehensible individual who can never be trusted!

We never actually understood what he was until we ran his background check under his proper legal name. He is the proud owner of at least four federal convictions, serving eight years of a ten-year sentence.

The convictions pertain to various criminal activities, including recent cases of diesel fuel tax evasion and involvement in the manufacturing and transportation of illicit drugs such as marijuana and possession of controlled substances. Had I known of his background and real name initially, he would never have been accepted as company pumper, certainly never project manager and VP of field operations.

All of Gil's abject lying has caused me and my company regulatory problems with the federal SEC, the Texas State Board of Securities, the Colorado Board of Securities, and the Washington State Board of Securities. However, in responding to Colorado, they, in turn, have focused their attention on Gil and his companies, leaving me alone. The state of Washington has served me and my companies with a judgment of $40,000 for the companies and $40,000 personally as well as $7,500 compensatory damages.

Gil began having client parties on the leases. He knew if I reverted the agreement since he wasn't paying the invoices and honoring his legal responsibilities, I would keep him and the clients off the leases with armed guards, and he couldn't have that. I was told that on his first client get-together, he had some rather unsavory individuals that weren't employees or clients hanging around him at his parties. He had his bodyguards because he knew what I was capable of. He had three parties. I understand the first one was the most elaborate. He rented a party venue and contracted with a motor coach company to have two buses to drive people around from lease to lease. They were all having a good time leg pissing me on their way from lease to lease, especially the bus with Gil on board. Gil videoed himself interviewing investors and bashing me with slanderous statements.

Gil and his abject lies and sabotage caused me regulatory issues with the SEC, the State Board of Texas Securities, and the Florida Securities Board.

The following is a list I compiled for my attorney to prove his lies to present to the authorities.

Partial List of Gil's Intentional Sabotage of My Companies Projects

1. Turned away oil transports when Pam called HF oil purchasers.
2. Oil was stolen from the state lease batteries, and lease batteries next to the state lease, and most likely the Highway 10 lease battery.
3. Slowed work on all projects to cause dissent between my company's staff and clients.
4. Work slowdown caused Highway 10 leases to lapse.
5. Created fraudulent invoices.

6. Created exorbitant invoices.
7. Emptied produced water from fracking jobs into Ox B-10 reserve pit and charged for water disposal and trucking of water to a disposal site while claiming he was dewatering and covering this pit. It was causing my company TXRRC fines and hiring an independent to do the job right (which still wasn't done right).
8. He continually performed needless work on the projects to create invoicing while not performing the work his companies were contracted and paid to do, such as putting wells into production.
9. Failed to complete the job tasks he was paid for and supply my company with field data reports for TXRRC.
10. Failed to put pumpjacks on projects my company paid for.
11. Encouraged other vendors to invoice excessively and label invoices incorrectly, showing labor and supplies that weren't performed.
12. Started defaming my company and myself to the marketing team at the company meeting in June of 2014 at his Midland office and conspiring with clients recruiting the Dream Team to bring suit against me.
13. Gil and the California attorney started communicating with staff and clients on conference calls approximately in Jan. or February 2015 about creating an agreement to take over my company's projects.
14. At the time of the above conference calls, Gil and/or the California attorney convinced the Dream Team to bring suit against my company and me to leverage the resolution agreement.
15. Admitted to the husband-and-wife marketing team in Florida that even though Patrick was paying debts for sub-contractor work billed to Gil's companies, Gil wasn't going to pay those invoices because he wanted to run my company out of business.

Partial List of Gil's Slanderous
Statements to Staff and Partners

1. Claimed I bought the home in Granbury for $1,500,000 cash with partner money.
2. Claimed I had several million dollars in offshore accounts funded with partner money.
3. Claimed I bought several personal items funded with partner money.
4. Claimed Patrick wasn't paying Gil or other vendors and that I was diverting monies owed for field expenses to myself.
5. Claimed there weren't any wells fracked on any project.
6. Claimed I (Patrick) stated that it was not possible to reenter the rework well on the Highway 10 project due to junk in the wellbore.
7. Claimed the drill deeper and or fracking invoices weren't spent for the intended purpose and that it was diverted to myself.
8. Informed partners that only $40,000 was spent on fracking (contradictory since Gil claimed my company didn't frack).
9. Told partners not to pay frack invoices as they were exaggerated (Gil sent my company an email in an effort to develop the amount for the fracking).
10. Claimed my company knowingly took partners that, in actuality, weren't qualified.
11. Coached partners to say defaming and slanderous statements about my company and myself on video that he posted on YouTube during the bus rides back from project sites during one of his investor parties.
12. Made claims to other vendors that my company did not pay its invoices. This started in mid-2014 after Gil started consulting on drilling.
13. Started defaming and slandering me and my company approximately from June of 2014 to the marketing staff and clients.

The above list was compiled as backup data for our attorney to prove Gil's conspiracy and intention to destroy my company with forethought and extreme malice as he didn't dare to build a team or an oil and gas business on his own; he had to steal mine.

Letter to The Dream Team

The following is a letter I sent to a fellow that was purported to be the person who turned me over to the Florida SEC. He was also a member of the Dream Team:

To: John,

The prime reason for writing you this is just to get this off my mind: I don't expect you to believe anything, and it doesn't concern me if you believe it or not. It is obvious to me that the entire group of you so-called Dream Team Investors conspired to unethically relieve me of what my wife and I worked so hard to build. Recently allegations have been presented to me that you or someone close to you allegedly made complaints to the Florida Office of Financial Regulations due to your disdain for Steve. This person still worked for Gil at the writing of this, the complaint was made after Gil, and I came to an agreement on the resolution agreement.

Obviously, a clear violation of the terms agreed to in the resolution agreement. I suspected you and the so-called Dream Team of conspiracy with Gil for several reasons. First, the weekly robocalls during the negotiation process with Len posing as a concerned investor giving updates clearly fraudulent behavior. Then there were the investor parties with Gil slandering and defaming myself and my company on video, along with the bus ride interviews of investors that clearly showed Gil coaching and leading their responses, all to defame me.

The Florida issue has caused me SEC problems, which you knew it would when the complaint was filed with the aforementioned regulatory agency. Again, a clear violation of our agreement of not initiating contact to create an investigation by a regulatory agency. How you could refer to yourself as a Christian is beyond me; I used to refer to people like you as a convenient Christian (if the occasion arose for you to appear Christian, that's how you acted). I now know people like you are just fake.

You believed Gil's lies about my purchase of a lake house to the tune of $1,500,000 using partner funds, offshore funds in the millions, cars, and several other personal purchases with partner funds, all of which are abject lies, and I can prove it all. You met with me during the drilling of one of the Highway 10 projects, and with your knowledge and experience in the oil and gas industry and the quality of our projects, you knew all too well that during the time frame, we were drilling, that cost was over-inflated, and the project cost was far over budget. My only way to have profited would have been derived from oil and gas production; However, you chose to believe absolute lies from an individual with multiple felony convictions with a ten-year federal prison stint. Had I known his actual name when we employed his consulting firm and his criminal record, I would never have allowed him access to our leases, much less a consulting job.

Gil's companies were paid in excess of $11,000,000 for his consulting and well site construction, quite exorbitant, but I was assured at that time reduction in field expenditures was guaranteed. As you can surmise, drilling companies were charging prime rates as were the other companies supplying required equipment and services. All told expenses exceeded the funds collected for all project funding, yet you and others choose to believe the lies of an individual with multiple felony convictions.

Sincerely,
Patrick

The Florida Visit

I contracted with a Florida attorney who used to work for the division of the SEC that I was being charged by, to represent me in the Florida SEC issue. As it turned out, this was a large mistake; all he could do was request more and more documentation production and bend to the SEC's every request since that is all the feds could do was want more information.

My wife and I flew out to Florida to meet with the Florida division in charge of the federal complaint. The complaint originated because Gil convinced my clients that his lies were factual and I was misrepresenting our projects and saying anything to get their investment dollars. In actuality, all of my data was confirmed with Texas RRC reporting and extremely impressive logging data. We expended our total energy for two months compiling data for the subpoena, and the incompetents just kept requesting more.

I instructed my Florida attorney to shut down all documentation production because there was no more to produce. When we showed up at the SEC for the deposition, they had a young attorney questioning me, and I could tell she had never done this before; she just didn't show much poise. During questioning, it didn't appear that any examiners were familiar with oil and gas projects. These were the people that were supposedly looking out for the investing public.

Their examiners were so incompetent; not only did they know nothing about the production side of things but they also didn't know a thing about the financial side either.

Several times, their supposed accounting expert asked me about project returns. Case in point, part of my memorandum stated, "Over the life of the project based on current production and current oil and gas pricing, it would be possible to get six times return on investment." He hammered me at least five different times. "Did anyone receive that amount?" I said no. He asked the same question many other ways. I have answered you, "How could anyone receive that sort of revenue? It wasn't the life of the project. It was only eleven months into the production life of the well project. Yet only eleven months into the well's production life. Why? You need to pull your head out and read." I also told him, "You don't know shit from sugar about oil and gas."

Four SEC examiners were in the room with me and my attorney. The examiner hammering me was a little bald fellow. I told him he had asked the same question over and over, and I answered, "I believe at this point, I am going to step out and take a few minutes."

He told me, "We will tell you when you can take a break."

I replied, "Why don't you come with me, curly, and tell me about letting me know when I can take a break."

At the end of the day, I ended up with a judgment exceeding $45,000,000, not for rescission to the partner clients, and a $7,000,000 disgorgement in fines all because I didn't file the exemption form on the Reg D. Their fines included the total funds we raised plus my personal contributions along with a 15 percent penalty. Reg D pertains to the feds' ability to get their hands on our money through fees. Many companies didn't file at that time, and to date, there are many more than before. Our memorandum was written by one of the finest attorneys in Dallas, who once took the SEC to court over my same issues and kicked their butt. The big difference between myself and the other company years prior was how much justice I could afford.

Pam and I spent two very long and boring days in the offices of SEC, and the young examiner never got around to questioning

Pam. I told them they had disrespected our time enough; we were headed back to Dallas, and they could question Pam via teleconference or figure things out for themselves. Two weeks after we returned to Dallas, they set up a videoconference in the Fort Worth Office of the SEC. Our attorney was present, and the same four incompetents were on video. Pam said it was an absolute waste of time, and these people were looking out for the private investor; what a joke they were.

The same had been the case for the Colorado Board all over a $44,000 investor that received our letter on the suit we filed on Gil to quote, "I'm tired of you two companies fighting," I responded, "How else do you expect me to protect your interest? You need to stop your bellyaching and let me do what I know to do. However, it appears Colorado has lost interest in me and is pursuing Gil and his companies."

What the little pissant investor didn't understand is my company was receiving at least twenty-five lawsuits, nine judgments, and several garnishments of our bank accounts all due to Gil ignoring the requirements of the resolution agreement and refusing to communicate with project partners and all vendors listed as outstanding debt to be paid by Gil's company. Also, he conveniently forgot about the partners voting my company out and Gil's company in via ballots that all signed off on.

Mediation

Since it was clear we would be required to go to mediation on my lawsuit against Gil, we selected an attorney in downtown Dallas to act as a mediator. The next step is going to mediation on the twenty-fifth of May 2016 over my lawsuit filed against Gil and his companies. I can only surmise that they set this date as close to the Memorial Day holiday only to delay any payment required for debt settlement to us. This little sawed-off pissant was an attorney Gil's legal team recommended since they were familiar with his so-called impartiality.

Before we began, I turned over half the mediation fee of $4,360 (a waste of money). My legal team, my wife, and an employee of mine were present on my side. Gil, his wife, his legal team, and one other person were present on his side. The day began with all of us gathering in this attorney's conference room, being schooled by the mediator like kindergarteners about not proving who has the biggest balls and agreeing on a settlement; this process wasted an hour. We all adjourned to our separate rooms.

An hour later, the mediator came back with the offer from Gil: "*Nothing.*" The typical mediation nonsense ensued in the back-and-forth game of offer counteroffer. I told the mediator I wouldn't tolerate the senseless waste of time of back-and-forth ridiculous offers from Gil, and it was clear that the mediator had a bias against me. We took time out for a lunch break. I told my legal team I should have been more cautious in accepting this mediator since he came recommended by Gil's legal team, and after lunch, I was walking.

They talked me into staying, probably because they would get more billable hours for their time. At the end of the day, my legal team and Gil's legal team convened in the mediator's office and came to a settlement of $76,000 for my company. My guys returned to me with that offer and told them to tell the other side to forget it.

They talked me into accepting the offer and urged me to accept since he wanted his fees to be paid. Since they knew I was running out of money and couldn't afford their fees to go to court again, not a testicle amongst them. All told, after expenses, I netted approximately $44,000. As a result, we could not continue with office expenses since we were not funding a project at that time and had no regular revenue. The net effect was that our office building was foreclosed on, and Pam and I were again forced to move to less expensive housing.

The homeowner of this place rented the home before it was ready for us to move in; it needed paint and deep cleaning; there was trash in the front and inside the house. The previous tenants left the home incredibly filthy, and several appliances needed repair or replacement. We later learned in April 2016 that he was accepting our rent payments and not paying his mortgage. We inadvertently discovered this fact. All that would prove to be a moot point as our money was running out from selling all our personal property and trying to pay office expenditures, ongoing corporate legal bills, and living expenses. Pam and I once again needed to lower our living expenses and moved to a home in Plano, Texas.

To further elaborate on the Granbury Lake home, it was a property we had planned to purchase and retire in after conducting drilling operations on the Highway 10 sites. As we owned a significant stake in the project and successfully verified several million barrels of producible oil through the Rock Vision Log, we believed that our ownership in this lease would secure a comfortable income for the rest of our lives. The home was quite an estate—a 6,500-square-foot two-story Mediterranean-style home on the lake with a pool, a 3,500-square-foot detached garage in the same design as the house, and a four-car attached garage. It had a three-stall boat dock in the same design as the house; upstairs, it had two bedrooms, two bathrooms, a game room, and a media center with a fireplace; downstairs, it had three bedrooms with bathrooms in each, a very spacious master overlooking the lake, a large walk-in shower in the master bedroom with a large walk-in closet, a custom office with a fireplace and built-in bookshelves and custom executive desk, and a half bath in the hall for visiting guest, all of this on five acres that was privately gated.

All that would prove to be a moot point as our money was running out again since Gil had stolen all oil production, and the money we got from selling our personal property was ending. I was trying to keep up with office expenditures, ongoing legal bills, and personal living expenses.

The Partners Learn the Truth

The following letter was sent to the partners as Gil was ignoring our resolution agreement:

Date: November 24, 2015
To: All JV Partners

Lately, my company has been getting calls from at least three or four of you every week with the same questions: "What is up with the projects?" and "When will I receive revenue?"

The resolution agreement was signed, votes were cast, and all project assets and control were transferred to Gil and his companies in mid-June 2015, so obviously, we have no idea how the field or production is progressing as my company has been completely out of the picture. Gil and his companies in Midland have violated our agreement by refusing to communicate with several of you and the vendors as we have been told they will not take your calls. The intent behind the agreement was for Gil to take over as operating manager, keep the wells producing, work with the vendors by paying them for work they claim to have completed, and send out updates and revenue to you regularly.

In a conversation I had with a field inspector of the Texas General Land Office, he has indicated to me that regular monthly reports are long overdue and that revenue has not been reported to the agency; however, when he was there approximately one month ago, he witnessed the pumpjacks were operational, and he observed production going to the tanks. Additionally, he had a Texas Railroad Commission field inspector with him who claimed he would seal the wells. The GLO inspector only has jurisdiction over the state lease; of course, the RRC inspector has jurisdiction over all Texas wells in his territory.

The vendors are being treated the same, so my company received a judgment that directly violates the resolution agreement signed and agreed to by Gil and his companies. The resolution agreement states that if there is a violation of this agreement, a "reversion clause" goes into effect, entitling the assigning company to be awarded all projects back as well as punitive damages. This agreement is available to you at your request so you can be informed about these matters. The management of the assigning company will seek counsel on the best procedure for initiating the reversion clause and install a trustee that the courts would approve to oversee the day-to-day operations with an impartial field crew until the entire matter is resolved.

Thank you,
Patrick

Next for Gil

Since it was clear my company needed to rescind the resolution agreement with Gil and his companies because he refused to abide by the terms of the agreement by not paying the vendors and issuing NSF checks to the partners for oil revenue, I needed to assign a licensed and bonded operator that I knew of to replace Gil. The fellow I chose for this was Sal, a young guy familiar with the oil and gas industry. His familiarity was somewhat limited to shallow wells, but I felt I could bring him along with my knowledge.

I took Sal to the Highway 10 site project lease and showed him the logs we had run. Sal replied the logs didn't show him much, and I responded that maybe he was not meant for this area because several wells tested over five hundred barrels of oil in a 4-hour test, and one did more than twice that amount. It wasn't long after we filed our rescission and TXRRC paperwork. Gil flipped out, probably in a drug-fueled rage. I invited him to court and told him to bring the funds I assigned to him when we signed our resolution.

The guy I put in charge of the operations started communicating with Gil. However, Gil claimed that I forged his signature on the legal paperwork for the RRC; of course, all documents were signed at my attorney's office with Gil and his representatives present. Sal and Gil agreed and had to pay Sal and me $170,000. I told Sal, "That was the easiest $85,000 you ever made." He replied, "Don't blame me for being a shrewd businessman."

I told him that was not shrewdness; that was screwing over a friend. The lesson here is never to do business with a friend—another example of a no-good deed goes unpunished.

Of late, I have been contacted by one of Gil's former employees, Ronnie, who informed me that Gil is currently under investigation by several agencies, one of which is the Florida Division of the SEC. I am positive about this because his Fort Worth attorney's firm informed us that Gil received a subpoena in June of 2016 from the Florida SEC. It was the same division we had to answer to. Gil was subpoenaed to appear as we had, but his punishment of $750,000 was like a bee sting on an elephant's butt compared to our fines exceeding $45,000,000 plus. Eight years later, these reprehensible SEC jackbooted thugs are reaching into my social security and taking $200 a month, like that will solve these government thugs' problems. Also, I have been informed the FBI is investigating Gil for white-collar crimes. Last but not least, the Texas Rangers are finally investigating him for oil field theft and illegal transportation of oil in a truck licensed only for water transportation.

The feds have also subpoenaed the crew he convinced to get on board with him, my former team leaders which there were about seven, and more than likely their salespeople, probably twenty or more. Gil had requested two years to pay all outstanding debt. As I told him then that it was up to him to negotiate, I reminded everyone that he had no honor and to file suit against him. I sent our resolution agreement to all vendors. Only a small percentage challenged me; the rest filed suit on Gil—about thirty companies.

One of his so-called Dream Team investors finally came to his senses and filed suit on him in Dallas County, charging him with fraud and conversion of investment funds finding their way into his pockets and paying for one of his children's college tuition. This Dream Team investor guy was one of my largest investors, and he realized Gil was actually the bad actor and not me.

This investor had at least 20 percent ownership in most of my projects, making his portion of the frack jobs quite substantial. He was also one of the litigants who initially pursued legal action against me. Furthermore, he is among the major investors who failed to pay their share of the frack invoices, influenced by the bad advice given by Gil. The frack jobs cost over $ 2,000,000 for the three wells, and I only received close to $177,000 for the invoices I sent.

Most recently, Gil and his entities are being sued by a very prominent hotel developer from Fort Worth for the same reason he was guilty of accusing my company. His flagrant disregard for the trust my clients placed in him, believing his lies and engaging in sabotage, overbilling for equipment he never delivered, and charging for labor that was never performed, led him to believe he could continue deceiving his way through life. I believe Gil's contempt for the law, rules, and regulations of the Texas RRC and the general laws of life and business will ultimately land him behind bars for the rest of his natural life.

Gil sold the previously mentioned company a lease that didn't exist, lied about the total acreage, and sold them my state-owned lease along with my acreage that bordered the state-owned property we had tremendous drilling success on. As typical with this slimeball, he schmoozed the other company that he was a gifted oil field consultant, knowing all there was to know about the West Texas oil patch. In actuality, he was very incompetent and had the proverbial wool pulled over the eyes of everyone. He finally got a judgment against him over $11,000,000. The court determined that Gil was unjustly enriched by selling property he was not entitled to nor paid for.

My company paid for all of the property Gil was claiming; after he stole these leases, it will be his responsibility to plug those wells as ordered by the TXRRC, a very expensive undertaking. It was evidenced by a Texas RRC hearing that neither Gil nor his company had a good faith claim and failed to establish any possessory rights in the mineral interest to any of the leases he sold. He had a TRO on him to maintain the status quo until the trial in December 2019, which Gil ignored and obstructed justice in any fashion. I don't think he ever paid the judgment. Hopefully, the company that prevailed on the judgment will continue to keep the judgment active.

Gil was so persistent in taking all my personnel that he hired my bookkeeper. This individual got caught stealing from my company. First, she ran a tax reporting service from her home office using my company card, supplying her company with office supplies. She later anointed herself as treasurer/controller, which typically requires an MBA degree with years of CPA experience. She was neither of those mentioned earlier and only qualified for general bookkeeping. Her hiring philosophy was friends and family; her daughter came first as a part-timer and later full-time, but her talents didn't show through when she became full-time.

Shortly after, her daughter's friend was hired to answer the phones, and the sister of the tax girl who had a graphics art degree and was the only one with value and talent. I later learned this crew was working thirty-five hours a week and being paid for forty, and additionally, the girls got the PMS time off that was time paid for. She also had her cousin there as office manager. She had a condition she was being treated for, so she wasn't full-time either but was being paid as such. I had my fill of her, treating my company like hers. She had extremely lax rules, and I paid the price for it. If any staff went over their thirty-five-hour week load, they got overtime. It wasn't until we changed our operating system software that we discovered her theft. She gave herself a pay raise. At one point, she paid herself $90,000 and friends and family over $50,000 yearly. I did clean house. The graphic artist was the only one I regret having to eliminate from the corporate payroll.

We had a hearing with the workforce commission over our company not paying unemployment for her. The outcome was that the examiner felt she had misappropriated company funds.

The following is an excerpt from the workforce commission agent:

> The evidence establishes that the claimant,
> in this case, was separated from the last work with
> this employer when she was terminated by the
> employer. The evidence indicates that the claim-
> ant gave herself a pay raise without authorization

and she failed to adequately perform her job duties. This appeal tribunal finds that the claimant's actions were in poor judgment, at least, and reflective of an intent to misappropriate the employer's finances. The claimant, in this case, clearly mismanaged her position of employment, which amounts to misconduct with work. A disqualification is in order under Section 207.044 of the act. The determination disqualifies the claimant without further need of the commission's attention.

The determination dated December 18, 2014, disqualifying the claimant under Section 207.044 of the act beginning November 30, 2014, will be affirmed.

This stupid bitch would, from time to time, just pay invoices without consulting me. I would just imagine she was doing that because a lot of the invoices were coming from Gil and his companies. She eventually went to work for him. I terminated her in late November and gave her four weeks' severance. My generosity was rewarded by her giving my corporate books to Gil after manipulating the accounting records to look like I had taken a lot of money without paying any corporate expenditures.

Partners Discover the "Real" Bad Actor

The following is a letter that one of the marketing crew put together and sent to all client partners along with proof of his criminal background and tax liens.

Dear partner:

The purpose of this letter is to make all of Gil's and Patrick's oil companies partners aware of a situation that affects all of us. As it turns out, we have all been duped and the subterfuge is continuing as I write this. I have been concerned for some time now with Gil and the promises that have been made by him. Additionally, I was concerned with the circumstances surrounding the takeover of Patrick's oil company's projects. Out of my growing concerns, I initiated an investigation. I shared my concerns and investigative results with others who had direct involvement with Gil who, in turn, have shared additional details with me as well as confirmed a few of the details, which the investigation established.

Gil, as he has been renamed for this book, has mentioned, in passing, that he had a drug charge well into his past. What he failed to mention is that there were *four* separate charges at four different times, all of which consisted of *felony* drug charges, including a separate *felony larceny* charge as well. He was convicted on all charges from the possession of illicit drugs to the manufacturing of illicit drugs.

Most of the drug charges fell under "penalty group 1," which is reserved for the worst illicit drugs out there. For his last charge, he was *still out on bond* from a previous charge when he was arrested yet again on a new charge. He was convicted on all occasions receiving as much as ten years' probation, and when he was arrested for the third and then fourth time, he was sentenced to eight years in prison. He apparently has spent eighteen years of his adult life committing crimes and serving time for them.

Unfortunately, as was reported to me early in the investigation, after only a cursory search, he has spent more years in prison than he has as an oil well operator. Apparently, his habitual criminal background brought him, once again, to a point where he saw an opportunity to take a short cut via manipulating, deceiving, lying, and stealing as it has paid off for him in the past. This appears to be who he really is and not the charming, good ole innocent boy that he intentionally and, through deception, portrays himself to be. It obviously works for his intentions of acquiring trust through deceit. Trust, it appears, is something he otherwise would be unable to earn.

To elaborate, in the beginning of Patrick's oil company, for the first few years or so, I recall everything seemed to be running smoothly and being relatively well managed. Then Patrick had a problem with his project manager, who had a drinking problem which eventually interfered with his duties and safety on the job sites. As a result, Patrick and he parted ways. Through word of mouth, Gil wound up contacting Patrick; and after asserting to Patrick what he could do for the company, when Patrick hired him. Gil began taking over the management of the wells and as a direct result of his reassurances and suggestions to Patrick, was entrusted with more responsibility. It was apparently during this time that Gil started getting "ideas" and told Patrick that he would be more than happy to start speaking with the partners and the marketing team as part of his responsibilities. Over time, he strategically positioned himself more and more, charming the clients as well as the marketing team. During this same time period, he began overbilling and double-billing Patrick. Being that there are so many projects and wells under each project, and pages upon pages of bills that were being submitted, it took time to decipher that this was occurring. At the same time, Gil started "confiding" in the partners that Patrick wasn't paying him. While this was not true, the partners and the marketing team had no way of knowing that and were growing concerned. In the meantime, Gil was being paid for the work that Patrick was able to verify and then Patrick began questioning the other billings which were bogus or grossly exaggerated. But during this same time, Gil was careful to stay friendly with Patrick and act as though he was being helpful to him, so Patrick had no idea and no reason to suspect what Gil was up to. Then Gil began telling the partners, again in confidence, as well as the marketing team that if he didn't get paid soon, he was going to refrain from any further work. During this period, clients started calling Patrick and making him aware of their concerns. It was at this well-orchestrated time that Gil approached Patrick and informed him that he needed to make Gil an officer of Patrick's oil company and that only under those conditions, along with a "cut" of the proceeds from partners, would he continue to work and "solve" all the problems of his oil company was now having. Patrick agreed in the best interest of the former oil company and the partners, or so he thought, and made Gil an officer of the former oil company. Gil was playing and manipulating both sides, lying to both sides and building animosity between both sides instead of using what he knew to help correct things, he used it to manipulate everyone and the situation to his own benefit. He feigned concern for the partners while complaining about them to Patrick and how unappreciative and demanding they were even though Patrick was doing everything he could to resolve all the problems.

Gil would then do the same with the partners, complaining about Patrick. This was all done unbeknownst to the partners and to Patrick.

Also, during that time, Gil was calling the marketing team individually and "schmoozing" them so shortly after Patrick made Gil an officer, Gil apparently had enough confidence now, so he began having second thoughts and decided since he was achieving all that he set out to and was winning over the marketing team, the ones who brought in the money in the first place, he could eliminate Patrick altogether and make more money if he completely "took over," "ran," and "controlled" the former oil company projects, the wells themselves, and Patrick's marketing team, thereby eliminating Patrick altogether.

During all this, Gil was pulled over by the feds, presumably due to his background, and they detained him as they suspected and confirmed that he was stealing a form of diesel that was very closely monitored due to its deeply discounted price. Perhaps, it could be equated with stealing food stamps. He claimed to the marketing team that he was doing it for Patrick's oil company— yet another one of his deceptive lies when, in fact, it was for his personal use as he bought the diesel at a fraction of the cost and resold it to Patrick's oil company at full price and pocketed the difference. So once again, he was arrested as this was a federal crime.

By this time, Patrick began isolating the gross "errors" in billing by Gil. He assumed they were simply "errors," as he referred to them, giv- ing Gil the benefit of the doubt since Gil was deceiving Patrick with his innocent act. Now that Patrick picked up on the errors, Gil had to come up with a new ploy to deceive. So around the same time, he started his own oil company, which was in late 2014, not 2009 as he states in his documentation, and he also started subbing out the work representing to Patrick that if he paid Gil directly, Gil would in turn distribute the monies to the subs and make sure billing was correct. Patrick went along and paid Gil directly. So now Gil was subbing out most of the work for which he was being paid directly by Patrick's oil company; only he kept the money and didn't pay the subs who then, justifiably, refused to continue working. Now the projects were standing still again. Partners were angry with Patrick due to what was being represented to them by Gil through the back door, and Patrick was at a loss. All of Gil's *plans and manipulations* were coming together. He even convinced, through his deceptions, several of the partners to help. Unfortunately, they thought they were acting in good faith as they truly had all the partners' best interests in mind, and Gil had duped them just like everyone else. Gil had carefully, meticulously, and with a well-thought-out plan laid the foundation for himself to take over the former oil company projects for his own benefit; and that's exactly what he did.

Alternatively, when all the money was going out for work that was not being completed, Patrick, in an attempt to save the company and at Gil's suggestion, requested additional funds from some of the partners that were on wells for which Gil advised Patrick that he needed to collect more money for the fracking that Gil was to do.

Patrick also gave up his personal shares of each project that he had set aside for himself and began selling them to help the company. That is not the behavior of someone that is looking to steal; that is, however, consistent with someone who is making a sacrifice to protect! To protect what he worked very hard for and sacrificed for projects that he and his company had built from the ground up!

Additionally, the investigation reflected that Drill Rig Consultants and Big Rental Equipment, Gil's "proclaimed" companies that he allegedly had during this period, are no longer in existence even though (1) Drill Rig was never his company to begin with (it belonged to someone from Odessa that used his office for an address) and (2) Gil still has those names on signs and further represented that he sold one-half interest in Big to a company by the name of OPM ("Other People's Money") out of Miami, Florida, not Colombia as he has misstated. When he actually sold the one-half interest, it was apparently due to the fact that he used the new partners' funds on deposit with his new company for attorney's fees to facilitate his plans to take over the former oil company projects and for his vacations and ran out of money. He bounced so many checks that he had to change banks. Insofar as attorneys are concerned, and he's been through quite a few, he represented to the attorneys that he never knew or agreed to his being added as an officer of the former oil company; however, his signature is on all the paperwork as now that he was taking over the former oil company projects due to "problems," being an officer would backfire and implicate him as well. So he denied that he knew. He's also not married but obviously thought that saying so painted a more trusting picture of him.

Kelli doesn't even live with him; he was with another woman some years ago before prison with whom he had children, but she terminated the relationship with him. He did have a relationship with a woman around the time of prison. However, due to her drug abuse and her extensive arrest record including child endangerment, he has the children from that relationship.

He has gone through employees of Big Rental like water after battling and fighting with so many of them, and they are very willing to share their experiences and opinions of Gil. Big was the only business that was ever previously his; a small equipment rental company. In speaking with a few members of his marketing team and former employees from Big Rental in Midland, apparently, Gil's lies are as prolific as his temper. He represented that OPM is a large oil company that is so large that it only takes clients that are interested in opening accounts in excess of $100,000,000. This is nonsense. He also released a short video to a few members of the marketing team of hitting oil that was passed onto at least one partner but then gave the order not to send out the video as it was a mistake and said "that well" belonged to his children and "not the partners." I don't think it's too hard to figure out what happened there. He also tries to portray himself as being worth millions. That is, he represented that at least to anyone *outside of Midland* who knows better and knows the real Gil—as a brokster.

Additionally, when work wasn't being completed after he took over Patrick's oil company projects, he told his new company partners that it was due to his working on the former oil company wells and then told the opposite to the former oil company partners. Now think about this: When we all bought a portion of ownership in a well, our first concern was getting back our initial investment as this represents our risk. No one should stop selling oil at any price until that's achieved. I mean, who knows with certainty where the price of oil is going and how long it will take, or for that matter, how long it will stay there? No one can see into the future. So why not take the risk off the table? That would make sense unless someone wants you to think it's not profitable. This was yet another outright deception. Gil does not report any flow rates to the TXRRC but is, in fact, pumping. His purpose is twofold. This way he can send the partners insignificant checks to keep them quiet; and at the same time, since he's not reporting the amount, he can pump a larger amount or any amount he wants for that matter. Who would be the wiser? Who knows how many thousands of barrels have really been pumped out of the thirty-plus wells? In one breath, he's claiming to the partners that oil is too low to sell, but then he's pumping just enough to get a ridiculously small check to some of the partners as others are told their checks went out and must have gotten lost really. He tells the partners he's pumping to keep the holes open this is ridiculous. Then why not pump enough to make it worth their while? This is just another one of his schemes so he can justify pumping even though he's not reporting it when in actuality he's pumping large quantities and then selling all of it, and let's try to imagine what he's doing with the overage that's not going to the partners. Again, this isn't too hard to figure out.

Then there are the recent changes within his new oil company that Gil's been talking about. They are not exactly what he has led partners to believe either. He has known everyone's backgrounds on his marketing team for well over a year now! There are no surprises for him the only surprise is for the partners and at least part of the marketing team with regard to Gil's background.

The partners and the marketing team were not aware of his true background consisting of numerous Felony arrests. I would imagine the marketing team would have had an issue with his background if they knew the details and the fact that he hid the true depth of his record. At least I would hope so. As for the recent changes, they were actually directed at covering the way his business is set up so the regulators can't go after him. Additionally, he has apparently exploited the situation and used the opportunity as an excuse to fire marketing members that are more knowledgeable and have been questioning Gil and backing him into a corner regarding all his many lies.

If, in fact, the attorneys were behind letting go of members of the marketing team due to their backgrounds, and if it were not just a ruse to take the attention away from Gil's background and why they were really let go, why then are there several habitual Felony offenders still on the marketing team and with the company? For that matter, why is Gil himself allowed with his extensive felony record? Oh, wait, it's because the company isn't even in his name. But obviously, that should still exclude any association by his new oil company with him, and that still doesn't explain why other Felons besides himself are still associated with the company. This represents just more lies and subterfuge to take the attention away from his background and what he was actually doing.

He also took several people off salary in his new plan and is giving them a "cut' of all partner monies that come in, in lieu of their former salaries. This way nothing comes out of Gil's pocket. In other words, he no longer has to pay those individuals a salary if money is not being raised and if money is raised; and he, therefore, has to pay them. He then will give them the promised cut of the partners' monies instead of going into his own pocket. One word: *shrewd*. He may not be the smartest or most educated book-wise. Reading his emails or simply listening to him speak confirms that, but he certainly thinks and schemes like an extremely streetwise criminal with no deficiencies. Another thought if the companies that Gil allegedly originally had were so successful when he took over Patrick's oil company projects, then why are they both out of business now? By the way, his new company, according to the state of Texas's Office of the Comptroller, forfeited its right to do business. Also, although his new oil company isn't in his name, it is in Kelli's name. But Drill Rig wasn't in his name either, or was it in Kelli's name? It appears that that company was using his address. So what did he really have before he brought his "Ponzi scheme" to fruition?

Nothing more than a small equipment rental company for a few years and an extensive criminal background.

It may be too late for those of us that started with the former oil company to get our money back. But at least in the new oil company he started, partners may be able to get refunds. I fully intend to forward this letter to every agency I can, but each additional letter or complaint will help expedite whatever process can be initiated. I'm sure he'll never see another penny from any of us because his so-called Dream Team marketing team has been unable to raise enough capital under his mismanagement to keep the company going since he continually used the partners' monies for his personal use. He obviously thought that the marketing team would be able to continually raise enough money, thereby allowing him to continually use the new monies to replace what he had misappropriated. He may think he's smarter than all of us, but I have news for him. He is anything but as smart as he thinks he is. As they say, the cat's out of the bag.

I sincerely wish each and every partner much luck and success in recovering what you can.

Most sincerely and God bless,
A fellow partner

Gil Meets the SEC

While compiling my book's data, I came across several emails from Gil. Perhaps the above letter's drafter should have mentioned his atrocious grammar and inability to write intelligent thoughts. Reading some of the progress reports he sent, I have a hard time understanding how any of the partners believed in him. The grammar wasn't easy to follow and made the flow of the report unintelligible.

While understanding a college degree isn't a prerequisite for successfully being a field consultant, at least a high school education helps when communicating with upper management and reporting project progress to partners. Some of the finest people I know don't have higher learning, but they are good people and are free from addictions to illegal, harmful substances.

In my initial meetings with him, his lack of a higher education wasn't apparent. I could tell that his experience in the field was obvious. I have changed my requirements for employing field personnel, knowing that a degree won't be required. I will, however, require an individual with higher learning as a requirement and additionally free from federal convictions. Evidently, Gil spent so much time with drugs and being incarcerated that he couldn't concern himself with an education.

Sometime after Gil and I formalized the resolution agreement, Ronnie discovered several disturbing facts about Gil. His past was filled with several felonies, and Ronnie noticed Gil was receiving several subpoenas being delivered to the office. It raised many questions in his mind that compelled Ronnie to investigate independently.

After he found out what a slimeball Gil was, Ronnie couldn't in good conscience continue his association with such a reprehensible person. Gil is also being investigated by the Washington State Board of Securities, the Colorado State Board of Securities, and the Texas State Board of Securities in addition to the Oklahoma State Board of Securities. Also, I have been informed that the FBI is investigating him for white-collar crimes. Last but not least, he is being investigated by the Texas Rangers for theft of oil. However, they don't seem to care about that either since we couldn't interest them about Gil's theft of our oil. Gil never made disclaimers in his offering memorandums about his felonious past, and the SEC doesn't appear to care about the omission of his past since that wasn't a talking point in their claims against him.

Also, being subpoenaed by the SEC are the sales staff that Gil recruited away—Chester, Charles, Jim, the husband-and-wife marketing team in Florida, the California sales guy, and most likely anyone connected to Gil and his companies—as the SEC wants their deposition on all sales made through Gil's company. It originally appeared the only ones responding to any subpoenas were the husband-and-wife marketing team from Florida. I later learned this wasn't the case. I heard Chester answered his subpoena and was quoted to have said, "I just used what Patrick put in writing on the PPMs." I have been informed the SEC is interviewing clients as well. I was also informed that Gil has several lawsuits against him and his companies for nonpayment of invoices. Some of these companies are the same ones that brought suit against my company. Several firms have default judgments against Gil and his companies—at least ten. The cases are all filed in Midland County with one coming from Hockley County. Being there are 254 counties in Texas, it would be extremely time-consuming to search them all for suits against him and his companies.

The case shows his flagrant disregard for the trust his clients place in him by overstating invoices and lying on invoices for equipment and labor never performed or purchased. His contempt for the law and general rules and regulations will ultimately land him behind bars, where he needs to spend the rest of his unnatural life.

He sold the previously mentioned company oil and gas leases that didn't exist, lied about total acreage size, and sold minerals in the state lease and their associated properties, along with the Leases that bordered my state lease and their associated properties after he had the leases taken away for not properly managing the leases and selling oil that the royalty owners weren't paid including my company's clients. As in his typical mode of operating, Gil schmoozed the plaintiffs into believing he knew all there was to know about well completion and the necessary equipment to go along with the production sites, when in fact, he wasn't as capable as he pretended to be, in our case we found this out far too late.

Gil had a final judgment against him and his entities over $11,000,000 from the hotel developer and their entities. Also, a trial had been set for the amount as mentioned above and the cause number. The plaintiffs also had a TRO against Gil that maintained the status quo for at least until February 19, 2019. The trial didn't happen until December 2019 when Gil was capable and willing to obstruct justice in any fashion.

The State Bar of Texas

As I had mentioned earlier, we filed a grievance with the State Bar Association against the attorney Gil assigned us for the resolution agreement. This scumbag attorney was as dirty as Gil. Unbelievably, an attorney can agree to judgments against anyone without the knowledge or approval of the company or person named as a defendant. We signed no agreement with the attorney in question; he was merely appointed to us as ordered under the resolution agreement. They clearly had an agenda against me. Gil's responsibility was to cover all costs incurred in my representation as the resolution agreement required. This scum of an ambulance chaser agreed to all sorts of negotiations with vendors that Gil was responsible for paying. One, in particular, garnished a bank account that had nothing to do with the previous projects that Gil was working on. The scumbag entered into several agreed judgments without my knowledge or consent, totaling well over $500,000. My representation during the resolution agreement wasn't worth the over $2,000 per hour I paid. It proves the high-priced downtown Dallas boys were just that *"high priced."*

The following is a letter I wrote to the Texas State Bar:

The following State Bar of Texas complaint
and the attorney in question's rebuttal, along

with our response to his rebuttal, are intended to validate our position about Gil's reprehensible behavior as was the case for his attorney, who was supposed to represent us.

Grievance Against the Attorney in Question

In June 2015, an agreement was made between my company and Gil's company at my Dallas attorneys' offices. This agreement was signed and agreed upon 108 and witnessed by all. Gil representing his company would take over the projects that my company had in Pecos County and operate them. {Agreement attached) On page 2 of the first amendment to the resolution agreement, Section 6 says Gil's company will indemnify Patrick's company and provide counsel should any suits develop. Gil and his company per the agreement hired the attorney in question located in Odessa, Texas, to be our counsel, but we later found out that he was also hired as counsel for Gil and his companies as well.

Our first issue with the attorney in question began with the equipment company's lawsuit (attached) this vendor is also mentioned in the debt list in the resolution agreement as well. The attorney in question entered into an agreed judgment with the equipment company, and the judgment says that Kelli and the attorney in question all appeared and agreed to this judgment. I was never made aware of this, never asked to appear, and never told about any negotiations.

I now have $210,000 due and owing (which a large portion of the invoice actually belongs to Gil's firm) to a vendor that Gil agreed to pay in the resolution agreement. I would never have agreed to this!

Our second issue with the attorney in question was in the investor lawsuit (attached). The attorney in question sent me discovery from this suit, which I filed my answers and sent them back to him on or about December 29. The attorney in question never turned in our responses to the discovery which made us automatically admit everything. I hired another attorney to help me and sent him proof that I had filed my questions and he reached out to the investor attorney, who was going to file sanctions on the attorney in question (email attached).

Our third issue was a surprise garnishment that hit all of my companies' bank accounts, even accounts that had nothing to do with this particular vendor. This event occurred on Friday, February 12, 2016. We had an employee at the bank tell us she could not do a wire because we had garnishments on our accounts. Again, we knew nothing about this problem or why or how we had our money seized. With Monday being a holiday and being unable to pay our bills and employees this was extremely frustrating! This vendor was an electric repair company and they were awarded a judgment, just another agreed judgment entered into by the attorney in question, Gil, and Kelli that we knew nothing about. No notice, no negotiations, or emails.

Our final issue is the most obvious and that is the lack of communication with the attorney in question, "our attorney." When the resolution agreement was signed and we had our first lawsuit, we sent the suit to the attorney in question. The only response he gave us was, "received thanks." There was never one phone call or any communication with him to us except when he sent us the discovery. No notice of judgments, requests to appear in court, no requests to agree to a judgment amounts whatsoever. The attorney in question, Gil, Kelli, Gil's company, and all other companies associated with Gil appeared and agreed to all these on our behalf; yet it was not on us any longer to pay them due to the resolution agreement and we would *never* have agreed to them.

The attorney in question has cost us time and money having to hire another competent attorney to help us out of the mess that he has created is absurd! The amount of frustration, anxiety, and monetary hardship he put upon us is reprehensible. A monkey would've been more efficient and organized, and this is a complete embarrassment not only to us his clients but to you as well, and my prayer is that you do not advocate these antics and would not let anyone else go through the emotional beating we have.

Thank you for your consideration.

I look forward to your response.

Response to Grievance Allegations— CDC State Bar of Texas

Dear Sirs/Madams,

After speaking with Mr. Smith, it appears that the central "finding" which may have led this grievance to be "determined" to be a complaint is that some "conflict of interest" existed between several parties subject to litigation and that Patrick's previous company. One of those parties has complained that my actions, as professional counsel, violated the standards of the bar due to said conflict. For the purposes of this complaint response, I assume that Patrick's complaint is simultaneously and contemporaneously a complaint by his company. This matter concerns my representation of his company pursuant to indemnification stemming from an asset purchase. Patrick sold certain assets and liabilities to Gil and his company. The "resolution" of the debts owed by Patrick's company was a duty delegated to Gil and his company pursuant to contract, and Gil had a certain time period within which to satisfy the debts, and Gil and his company had a full delegation of settlement authority within the agreement (full authority to "settle" or dispose of litigation, creditor claims, debts, etc.). (c) A lawyer shall not permit a person who recommends, employs, or pays the lawyer to render legal services for another to direct or regulate the lawyer's professional judgment in rendering such legal services (Tex. R. Prof Conduct 5.04). Ultimately, the complaint can be reduced to this: Patrick and his company delegated its authority, in contract, to settle, dispose of, govern, or control litigation resulting from the liabilities of Patrick's company. Gil and his company then delegated said authority to me Weasel (the attorney in question) for any and all representation of Patrick's company's debts which were previously assumed by Gil and his company. Weasel (the attorney in question) then exercised said authority in "agreeing" to allow certain debts subject to litigation to be reduced to judgment. Did Weasel (the attorney in question) violate rule 5.04 by allowing Gil and his company to "direct" or "regulate" his professional judgment in representing Patrick's company?

The answer is no because Weasel (the attorney in question) did not "permit" such a direction, but rather, Patrick "permitted" "another to direct or regulate the lawyer's actions in rendering legal services.

Weasel (the attorney in question) is not the "permittee." To aid the CDC, please take note of provisions in the "Assumption and Indemnity Agreement" attached hereto as Exhibit A. Now, THEREFORE, for good and valuable consideration, including the mutual covenants and agreements set forth herein, the receipt and sufficiency of which are hereby acknowledged.

Gil and his company hereby assumes and agrees to defend, indemnify and hold harmless the parties from and against (i) all indebtedness to be paid by Gil and his company pursuant to Section 2.4 of the resolution agreement; (ii) all liabilities other than indebtedness or contractual liabilities arising out of the ownership or operations of the assets transferred under the resolution agreement (but not out of the raising of capital for such operations or noncompliance with federal securities laws or tax laws) prior to, on, or after the closing date in the ordinary course of oil and gas operations; (iii) the vendor litigation (as defined in the resolution agreement), Patrick's oil company v. a company laying claim to leases district court of Tarrant County, Texas (to the extent provided in Section 2.8 of the resolution agreement), and the threatened claims by David an investor; provided, however, with respect to the vendor litigation (as defined in the resolution agreement), (a) Gil and his company may designate counsel to defend such litigation, (b) Gil and his company may direct the conduct of such litigation, (c) Gil and his company may control the settlement of such litigation, and (d) parties will cooperate with the defense of such litigation. Additionally, even in such case as Weasel (the attorney in question) "did permit" the payor (Gil and his companies) to direct the outcome of the litigation, Weasel's (the attorney in question) "professional judgment" was directed by the contract between the parties and not by the Payor. Therefore, Weasel's (the attorney in question) "professional judgment" was directed by Patrick and his company pursuant to contract.

This arrangement is similar to rulings governing the "professional judgment" of insurance companies and their hired attorneys. And we have noted that "an insurer's right of control generally includes the authority to make defense decisions as if it were the client 'where no conflict of interest exists'" (Rule 1.06 of the Texas Disciplinary Rules of Professional Conduct, *Unauthorized Practice of Law Comm. v. Am. Home Assur. Co.*, 261 S.W.3d 24, 42 [Tex. 2008]). I would also suggest that these parties' "interests were aligned" and "no conflict of interest" existed because in the state of Texas, "delay for the sake of delay" is not a valid purpose for denying litigation (other than a general denial), and the Judgments taken were taken with the aim of reducing the opposing party's claim for attorney's fees. The party "adjacent to" Patrick had an equal desire for the Judgment to be rendered at the lowest possible level. Patrick has failed to state how Weasel's failure to deny a claim in bad faith is synonymous with "contrary to interest." Patrick may argue that affirmative defenses to these debts existed; however, after ongoing requests from Gil's company for documents and information regarding claims, Patrick presented no such defenses (and in fact, his actions suggested that he preferred all such defenses to be presented by Gil's companies.

Further, as to the postjudgment disposal of any judgment taken, Weasel (the attorney in question) exercised his professional judgment under the impression that the "assets" of Patrick's company were controlled and/or possessed by Gil and his companies (the party subject to judgment). If certain assets subject to seizure, garnishment, or forfeiture were in the possession of the complainant, such is a civil claim for negligence damages, not a concern of ethical considerations found within the Disciplinary Rules of Professional Conduct. Further, Weasel's professional judgment at the time was guided by the belief that the Judgment would be satisfied by Gil and his company, that no undue consequences would pass to Patrick's company, the client, and that no conflict existed.

Hindsight may provide for civil arguments in this instance, but again, the professional judgment was sound. Finally, and most importantly, this particular "conflict of interest" was waived between the parties, both explicitly upon the advice of Weasel's counsel, and through contract: (1) all parties were aware of the conflict of interest prior to Weasel's representation; (2) Weasel's office specifically discussed, verbally and in writing, the conflict between the parties, and requested a waiver (Exhibit B); (3) the "entity" directing Weasel's professional judgment in rendering the legal services for indemnification was the party with "delegated authority" to make decisions concerning the litigation (a provision of which the complainant was previously aware); and (4) the complainant has failed to state what conflict of interest existed or what "interest" was not aligned with the interest of Weasel's Payor. (1) A lawyer may represent a client notwithstanding a conflict of interest prohibited by § 121 if each affected client or former client gives informed consent to the lawyer's representation.

Informed consent requires that the client or former client have reasonably adequate information about the material risks of such representation to that client or former client. Restate 3d of the Law Governing Lawyers, § 122 (3rd 2000). My payors sent notice to all creditors directing them to remit communications regarding Patrick's company debts to my office. My representation began after the signing of a "waiver of conflict of interest" between Patrick and Gil in August of 2015. Finally, while Patrick's negligence claims concern professional malpractice and not misconduct, I will attempt to handle Patrick's complaints against me for professional negligence in order:

1. Patrick seems to believe that my client and my office both agreed that I was officially Patrick's "counsel of record" in all litigation pertaining to his agreement with Gil and his companies. This is simply not true. My office entered as attorney of record in certain lawsuits according to the instructions of my client. Nothing more, nothing less.

2. The first lawsuit was filed in January of 2015, seven months prior to my representation

of Gil and his companies. My office never made any entry as counsel in the lawsuit, and my office never represented to Patrick or his company that he was represented in said lawsuit by my office. As to whether Patrick and his company should or should not have been indemnified by my clients, that is a third-party issue. Patrick claims that he "demanded indemnity" from my office (in December, after the judgment). Again, his agreement for indemnity concerns a third party (my clients) and not my office.

3. The electric contractor suit. My office made an entry as counsel in this lawsuit to defend against a debt. After my client indicated that the amount was just (or that no substantial defense existed), my client then authorized me to exercise full settlement authority (as provided for in the resolution agreement), and an agreed judgment was taken in exchange for a reduction in attorney's fees. My understanding as to the satisfaction of the judgment at that time was that my client was responsible for satisfying the judgment. I understand that my client failed to satisfy the judgment and that subsequently Patrick and his company had his bank accounts garnished. If Patrick feels that the "garnishment of his accounts" was the result of my professional negligence, I would direct him to the Resolution agreement and the obligations of my clients.

4. The water hauler contractor is the next suit. I received notice of this lawsuit and a demand for indemnity from Patrick's counsel on December 1, 2015.

In November 2015, my client verbally, and in writing, indicated that they no longer desired for my office to make an appearance on behalf of Patrick and his company and that they were denying the request for indemnity. Therefore, no entry as counsel in that matter was ever made by my office. I did acknowledge receipt of the documents with the phrase "RECEIVED."

5. I received notice of an additional lawsuit and a demand for indemnity from Patrick's counsel on December 1, 2015. In November 2015, my client verbally, and in writing, indicated that they no longer desired for my office to make an appearance on behalf of Patrick and his company and that they were denying the request for indemnity. Therefore, no entry as counsel in that matter was ever made by my office. I did acknowledge receipt of the documents with the phrase "RECEIVED."

6. David the investor. I did not represent any of these parties (or know of their existence) on February 2, 2015. My office made an entry as counsel in this matter on September 28, 2015 (my client agreed to indemnify Patrick and his company). Patrick is incorrect. No sanctions were filed against my office OR against Patrick OR against his company. You will note that sanctions were filed against Gil and his companies, and therefore this matter concerns Patrick in no way whatsoever. However, as a sidenote, it was Patrick's own attorney that caused substantial confusion in that case by indicating that he would be withdrawing as counsel

for Patrick's company (yet he remained in representation of his company).

If your office finds that this matter needs additional clarification, you will see a more in-depth explanation in the letter attached hereto as Exhibit C.

7. Patrick has complained about a "lack of communication." For any and all lawsuits for which I acted as attorney of record on behalf of his company, I entered such representation under the direction of my clients, the owners of the liabilities subject to litigation. If communication with Patrick was necessary, as it was in a few discovery instances, Patrick chose to act through his counsel of record, Stephen. There were several instances where responses to discovery against Patrick and his company were sought through Stephen's office. I am not sure as to what other "damage" Patrick believes this arrangement caused other than that he is unhappy with the outcome of his agreement with my clients.

8. Patrick has alleged that "Weasel (the attorney in question) cost us over $250,000 in judgments, liens, garnishments, and attorney fees as we had to hire another competent attorney to help us out of the mess Weasel created!" I am not certain as to any factual basis for this statement. "Weasel" was not the debtor party to any of the subject judgments, "Weasel" was not the party assuming responsibility for Patrick and his company's liabilities under the resolution agreement, and therefore "Weasel" cannot be responsible for accumulating these

debts. If Patrick is alleging that "Weasel" could have acted differently as counsel in order to "delay the adjudication" of Patrick's companies' debts, I would humbly suggest that attorneys in the state of Texas are not allowed to "delay for the sake of delay," and further that my office took all actions subject to the directions of my clients Gil and his companies.

9. Patrick's dissatisfaction with the arrangement of indemnification was an issue raised by my office prior to any representation whatsoever, specifically because I anticipated such a complaint. I believe his complaints are with my clients, and not with my office. Further, there is already ongoing litigation between Patrick and Gil regarding "failure to defend and indemnify."

I drafted the following letter as a rebuttal in response to the attorney in question responding to the state bar.

To: Investigator in Charge
Ref: 201601940
Date: May 18, 2016

Dear sir,

This letter will serve as a rebuttal of Weasel the attorney in question response to our grievance. He alleges that Gil and his company had a full delegation of settlement authority over my company within the scope of our resolution agreement with Gil and his companies. This statement as he proposes it is absolutely false. There was never an agreement to settle claims to the detriment of my company and no such authority was afforded Weasel the attorney in question to govern or control litigation to the extent my company would be responsible for debt payment. As stated in the agreement between my company and Gil's companies, the assignees were responsible for all indebtedness and were required to defend, indemnify, and hold harmless the assignors, so his statement Patrick "permitted" another to direct or regulate the lawyer's actions in rendering legal services is an absolute fabrication of the truth, this would only apply to his clients, Gil's companies; otherwise, why would I allow my company transfer certain assets to Gil and his companies and still end up with all the liabilities and none of the assets?

Weasel claims Gil and his companies had a full delegation of settlement and later, in his response, claims his professional judgment was directed by my company somewhat contradictory as much of his response letter is. Weasel also suggests the party's interests were aligned and that no conflict of interest existed this of course is false. In an email to my counsel for my company during the resolution agreement with the firm representing myself and my companies, Weasel (the attorney in question) admits there do exist conflicts of interest. That judgments were taken with the aim of reducing legal fees, why my company would be concerned about Gil's companies' attorney fees is beyond me. He never once enjoined Gil and his company as codefendants so any judgment would be the responsibility, indemnification, and defense of Gil and his company. Additionally, if there were an unbonded judgment entered against my company this would be a breach of the resolution agreement. With this said Weasel (the attorney in question) was well aware that his client was failing to indemnify since there were so many judgments being rendered against my company. He even states further in his response that he did not understand why his clients were not indemnifying my company.

Weasel also makes the ludicrous statement that he exercised his professional judgment under the impression that the assets of my company were controlled and or possessed by Gil and his company. If the assets were controlled by the aforementioned why would those assets be in my company's bank accounts? It is shocking that someone of Weasel's educational background would make such a ridiculous statement, it is clear this statement is nothing more than an attempt to defer from his misconduct. He also claims that his judgment was guided by the belief that Gil and his company would satisfy the judgment, and undue consequences would not pass to Patrick's company. I have no idea what judgment he refers to; there are at least nine judgments and at least twenty-five lawsuits due to his client's noncompliance with the resolution agreement. Weasel (the attorney in question) was well aware that his client was not indemnifying my company.

As he stated, he didn't know why his client wasn't indemnifying Patrick's company. He never notified my company concerning any judgment within the allotted thirty-day timeframe so we could provide our own defense, yet in every instance he either made a settlement as to an agreed judgment to the detriment of my company or absolutely failed to appear for court-ordered appearances rendering default judgments against my company.

The attorney in question also states his clients verbally and in writing no longer desired his office to make an appearance on behalf of my company. He knew the resolution agreement made a requirement of defense for my company and that nonrepresentation created a breach of agreement. Additionally, Weasel never submitted a motion to withdraw as counsel as required to submit.

Weasel (the attorney in question) claimed that he was not counsel of record in all litigation; this statement also is absolutely false, and as per the resolution agreement, legal representation was required. My company was to be indemnified and defended in any litigation; he even states in a letter to a Collin County judge that his office was serving as counsel of record for all defendants. Weasel also claims he is not certain that there is any factual evidence as to his representation costing my company over $250,000. After further review of the amounts of judgments, I discovered the amount of damage was greater than originally thought, these amounts exceed $800,000. If the attorney in question would just use common sense and look at the judgments, he would see the actual cost. My company never requested that Weasel delay for the sake of delay any adjudication of my company debts. As per the resolution agreement, these debts were the responsibility of his clients; once again, he makes contradictory statements that he was taking direction from Gil and his companies when earlier in his response he claimed he was taking direction from myself and my company.

Since there was no communication with my company's office from the attorney in question how could my company give any direction?

In closing, reading Weasel's response letter indicates his ability to fabricate a story that resembles nothing close to the truth. He contradicts himself several times in his letter which makes it very clear he was attempting to dig his way out of the hole he was burying himself in. He admits he was aware his client was not indemnifying my company, yet he continually subjected my company to agreed judgments and default judgments, how then could he say my dissatisfaction with his representation of my company actually lay with his clients when he suborned his client's breach of contract behavior.

Since backup data was provided with our original complaint and the attorney in question provided some emails, which by the way seem to only confirm our complaint we won't be including with this rebuttal, however, at your request, we can send it later if needed. I also notice that Weasel enclosed documents titled "Notice of Conflict: Request for Acknowledgement and Disclaimer." It appears that Larry (by the way a California atty) drafted these ridiculous documents, then transferred them to Weasel's coat-of-arms letterhead, ones that I never knew existed, more than likely because my legal representation would not agree with; they obviously were never signed. The attorney in question has created more problems than he solved especially since he made agreed judgments on several lawsuits without my consent, knowledge, or approval and failed to appear for court-ordered dockets, causing default judgments (all of these previously submitted as evidence) all to the liability of my company.

The following have been enclosed only to point out that the attorney in question did not adhere to the code of ethics as prescribed by the State Bar of Texas, not to be pretentious.

According to the Rules of Conduct

1. A lawyer is a representative of clients, an officer of the legal system and a public citizen having special responsibility for the quality of justice. Lawyers, as guardians of the law, play a vital role in the preservation of society. The fulfillment of this role requires an understanding by lawyers of their relationship with and function in our legal system. A consequent obligation of lawyers is to maintain the highest standards of ethical conduct.

2. As a representative of clients, a lawyer performs various functions. As advisor, a lawyer provides a client with an informed understanding of the client's legal rights and obligations and explains their practical implications. As advocate, a lawyer zealously asserts the client's position under the rules of the adversary system. As negotiator, a lawyer seeks a result advantageous to the client but consistent with requirements of honest dealing with others. As intermediary between clients, a lawyer seeks to reconcile their divergent interests as an advisor and, to a limited extent, as a spokesperson for each client. A lawyer acts as evaluator

by examining a client's affairs and reporting about them to the client or to others.

3. In all professional functions, a lawyer should zealously pursue clients' interests within the bounds of the law. In doing so, a lawyer should be competent, prompt, and diligent. A lawyer should maintain communication with a client concerning the representation. A lawyer should keep in confidence information relating to representation of a client except so far as disclosure is required or permitted by the Texas Disciplinary Rules of Professional Conduct or other law.

4. A lawyer's conduct should conform to the requirements of the law, both in professional service to clients and in the lawyer's business and personal affairs. A lawyer should use the law's procedures only for legitimate purposes and not to harass or intimidate others. A lawyer should demonstrate respect for the legal system and for those who serve it, including judges, other lawyers, and public officials. While it is a lawyer's duty, when necessary, to challenge the rectitude of official action, it is also a lawyer's duty to uphold legal process.

Rule 1.03. Communication

a) A lawyer shall keep a client reasonably informed about the status of a matter and promptly comply with reasonable requests for information.

b) A lawyer shall explain a matter to the extent reasonably necessary to permit the client to make informed decisions regarding the representation.

Comment: The client should have sufficient information to participate intelligently in decisions concerning the objectives of the representation and the means by which they are to be pursued to the extent the client is willing and able to do so.

Finally, this brings me to the point made in our original complaint that the attorney in question has not conducted himself professionally but, by his own actions, admissions, and arrogance, committed professional misconduct, how else could an attorney take direction from one party and make another party liable without ever notifying or getting the others' consent and approval; this, on the surface, seems illegal. Every agreed judgment and default judgment rendered against my company was due to his irresponsible actions.

In June 2015 we entered an agreement in good faith with Gil; we held up our end and turned over leases that were producing and in turn, we expected him to do the same. Nearly a year later, we have had a garnishment, liens, and judgments against us that have cost us money we did not have, time to fight these as we were supposed to be indemnified according to Gil's end of the agreement. Gil's company appointed the attorney in question to indemnify us in any litigation that arose.

As our appointed attorney by Gil and his companies, the attorney in question did not use the highest standard of ethical conduct, nor did he follow any of the rules that are mentioned above—first by taking on the responsibility of indemnifying my company as per the resolution agreement, by putting Gil and his companies needs ahead of ours, and then by having us sign a waiver of conflict without giving us full disclosure as to all the ramifications. Weasel never communicated with us about any of these cases; he did not turn in our discovery in the investors' case; and the only reason we hired Stephen was because Weasel never contacted us by phone to speak with us. We knew we had to pay money for an attorney that would help us out of the judgments, liens, and garnishment due to Weasel's neglect. His assumption was that we gave up all power to Gil and his companies, and to him to settle everything is preposterous. No one would enter an agreement and give up leases that were producing oil and giving us income only to defend ourselves from all the debt they failed to take care of. No one would sign over complete power to an attorney and opposition to settling things on their behalf without being consulted. His assumptions just don't make sense; they are just excuses for his neglect and in no way reflect the rules of conduct he is supposed to uphold but rather gross injustice, negligent, corrupt, and immoral.

By: Patrick

Any attachments or examples mentioned in any of my letters were included with the original letters at the time I sent them but won't be included with the book for reasons of privacy.

We Are Here

Being in the oil and gas business for the past thirty-eight years, I have been involved with and managed over four hundred drill sites. My training started with structural engineering, designing the telescoping derricks of the mobile drilling rigs for the first ten years. For the past twenty-eight years, I have been heavily involved in geological research to determine the best possible area and field to develop, well placement, and well completion. I have seen several companies, some of whom had the highest degree of ethics and integrity. However, many couldn't spell integrity. Not to toot my own horn, but I have always had the partners' interest at heart. Starting years ago, I drilled five shallow wells with my first offering for private investors. All wells hit and were completed; they weren't much to speak of but did produce enough to pay most of the investment back.

I started marketing projects for companies with fairly impressive marketing material; however, these projects were being sold by larger groups, not leaving me much to do with the deals. Charlie and I were selling projects for a guy with very impressive deals and good-looking science, but we weren't making much money. Charlie read an ad in the newspaper that Jack was looking for business partners, and we decided to meet with him not long after we started our own company. Jack never had access to leases with much intrigue, so we created our own by putting our heads together and adding as much science as possible from public geological reports and, later on, getting a graphic artist to design maps.

When I started the Permian Basin projects, I had a graphic artist with a geological and technical background that understood my write-ups. He created topographical, structural, seismic, and location maps showing offsetting locations with initial production rates higher than most wells in the immediate area.

The more I drilled, the better our maps looked. I had impressive initial production rates that I could show on our maps leading anyone interested in oil and gas investing to the decision that this area had the strongest locations. I did several projects in the Permian and had great success hitting all our wells with only two being slightly marginal. I had several thousand acres in Pecos County, one location I wanted to reenter a well on, that Gil later claimed belonged to his family. The well he reentered had extraordinary wellhead pressure creating a massive blowout that took over twenty-four hours to get under control. As it turns out, it was better to have Gil lay claim to this lease, and the RRC demanded lease reclamation. The more wells I did, the more he decided ownership should go to his company, and he even made a statement on video at one of his partner group parties that he couldn't let some "out-of-towner" have ownership in such an outstanding field. What a stupid statement to make to a group of investors where all the partners in attendance were "out-of-towners." It seems the stronger you build something, there is always someone who wants to take it away. Could it be that they don't have what it takes to build their own company, no guts or faith in themselves? Guys like Gil didn't have what it took to create a deal on their own?

Patrick was raised in the oil and gas business. His father was in upper management of the Sinclair Oil Company. He spent much of his life in Tulsa, Oklahoma, and was involved in go-kart racing and later on in auto racing. He always had an interest in structural design and drafting of welded structures.

After serving in the military during the Vietnam War, Patrick studied structural engineering in college and began designing telescoping oil rig derricks for a company in Tulsa, Oklahoma. Shortly after designing rig derricks, Patrick got involved in insurance company management, and later, he was recruited to move to the Dallas, Texas, community to manage a team of individuals in an oil company drilling horizontal oil wells in South Texas. Patrick excelled in oil well placement and oil well completion and developed his own oil and gas well exploration and production company. He is married and has two daughters and seven grandchildren. He also has two beautiful German shepherds.